GEORGE S. CLASON'S

THE
RICHEST MAN
IN BABYLON

GEORGE S. CLASON'S

THE
RICHEST MAN
IN BABYLON

A 52 BRILLIANT IDEAS INTERPRETATION
BY KAREN MCCREADIE

First published in 2009 by
Infinite Ideas Limited
36 St Giles
Oxford
OX1 3LD
United Kingdom
www.infideas.com

A CIP catalogue record for this book is available from the British Library

ISBN 978-1-905940-97-4

Designed and typeset by Cylinder

BRILLIANT IDEAS

INTRODUCTION

In 1926 George S. Clason issued the first of a famous series of pamphlets on thrift and financial success, using parables set in ancient Babylon to make his point. These were distributed to millions and were eventually published together as *The Richest Man in Babylon*. Since then millions of copies have been sold and the book has become a modern inspirational classic.

I think it's only fair to warn you that you probably wouldn't like the secrets to wealth he unveils. By all accounts, *The Richest Man in Babylon* is the antithesis of modern society. If quick-fix, magic-bullet philosophies are more your style (even though you know in your heart they don't work) then you'll probably be disappointed. If work is a four-letter word and you think delayed gratification is a sexual dysfunction then it might not float your boat.

The Richest Man in Babylon doesn't offer overnight solutions but the methods put forward for paying off debt, generating income and building wealth are as valid and applicable today as they were over 8000 years ago in Babylon. And those guys knew a thing or two about money.

In the pages of history there is no city more glamorous than Babylon. Its name conjures up visions of wealth and splendour and yet it was located beside the Euphrates River in a flat, arid valley. There were no forests, no mines – not even stone for building – but despite those challenges Babylon rose up from the desert as an outstanding example of man's ability to accomplish great achievements regardless of circumstance.

In some ways Babylon was like a modern day Dubai. The geographical locations for both centres of wealth were not great, and yet their ingenuity (and preposterous financial resources) made the impossible possible – although building a map of the world in the ocean by creating land and shaping it so the super-rich can buy their own 'country' is a bit more ostentatious, and certainly a lot less practical, than the Babylonians' achievements.

Archaeological expeditions funded by European and American museums have discovered that the Babylonians were an educated and enlightened people. So far as written history goes, they were the first engineers, astronomers, mathematicians, financiers and the first people to have a written language. The excavation of Babylon unearthed entire libraries containing hundreds of thousands of engraved clay tablets and it is this information that forms the basis of what we know about the Babylonians nowadays. Their accomplishments defy belief even today. The walls that surrounded Babylon, for example, were reported to be nearly fifty metres high (that's equivalent to a fifteen-story office building), up to eighteen kilometres long and wide enough for a six-horse chariot to patrol the top. The inner walls protecting the royal family's palace were even higher, and irrigation systems transformed the arid valley into an agricultural paradise.

Babylonians were clever financiers and traders. So far as we know, they were the original inventors of money as a means of exchange, promissory notes and written titles of property, so who better to teach us a thing or two about wealth?

This book will take 52 of the most important or interesting points from Clason's original and give them a modern twist so we can recognise the continued relevance of his advice. Whether you're in a financial pickle and find yourself up to your neck in debt, are concerned about your future because you have no savings or whether you just want to work out a system to regain some control over your money, then the wisdom contained in *The Richest Man in Babylon* is timeless.

1 LET REBELLION SWEEP YOU TO CHANGE

In the opening chapter, *'The Man Who Desired Gold'*, Clason tells us the story of Bansir, the chariot maker. He is telling his friend Kobbi about a dream he had where he was wealthy. But, *'When I awoke and remembered how empty was my purse, a feeling of rebellion swept over me.'*

This feeling of rebellion is a potent force for transformation and often acts as a flash point or point of no return. Bansir is finally angry; he's finally realised that despite years of diligent service and hard work he still has no gold in his purse. And it is this emotion that propels him toward financial transformation.

DEFINING IDEA...

To change one's life we must start immediately and do it flamboyantly. No exceptions.
~ WILLIAM JAMES.
PSYCHOLOGIST AND PHILOSOPHER

This is the magical moment of realisation when enough is enough. Something has to change and the only person that can change it is you. Many personal development speakers talk of this point, and one of the most famous of them is Anthony Robbins. He talks of his own flash point when he found himself broke at the age of twenty-two. He was living in 'a 400-square-foot bachelor apartment and washing dishes in the bathtub'. Overweight and miserable he hit the wall – he was filled with the rebellion that Bansir talks of – and made a commitment to himself that he would turn things around.

And turn them around he did. Today Anthony Robbins is the head of several very successful businesses, he coaches some of the most powerful people in the world, his seminars are attended by millions and he is wealthy beyond most people's imagination.

Everything we do, we do for a reason. Those reasons are either to achieve pleasure or avoid pain. The reason the flash point is so potent is that we will always do more to avoid pain than we will do to achieve pleasure. This is obvious when you consider our survival instinct. It is often in our darkest hour that we are forced into action because the desire to survive is extremely strong, and we are forced into fight or flight response to get out of danger and away from the pain. So if, like Bansir, you've reached your own point of no return, then get excited – change is in the air.

Unfortunately, for many people things never get that bad... I always remember a friend telling me about her relationship: 'It's not good enough to stay but it's not bad enough to leave.' All too often we don't reach the rebellion of the flash point for the same reason. The situation isn't that bad – we are in a no-man's land of inaction. There is no pleasure, but there isn't enough pain to motivate a change. If you want to change your financial fortunes then the quicker you hit the tipping point the better.

HERE'S AN IDEA FOR YOU...

If your financial position isn't really that bad but it's still not anywhere near what you'd like, then you need to get some leverage. Take the rocking-chair test. Imagine yourself at eighty explaining to your five-year-old granddaughter the regrets you have. What did you miss out on, how did it affect those you love? Use those feelings to propel you to action.

2 BIRDS OF A FEATHER FLOCK TOGETHER

Bansir is confused by his situation and says to his friend, 'We have earned much coin in the years that have passed... After half a lifetime of hard labor, thou, my best of friends, hast an empty purse... I admit that my purse is as empty as thine. What is the matter?'

DEFINING IDEA...

'Tis the only comfort of the miserable to have partners in their woes.

~ CERVANTES, SPANISH AUTHOR

Part of the problem is down to the fact that birds of a feather flock together. As human beings we decide what is acceptable and 'normal' by looking at the people around us. That means that our parents, teachers and friends exert huge influence over what we believe is possible in our lives. The upside is a feeling of belonging. The downside is that if we try to break out of those accepted paradigms we invariably meet resistance.

There is a famous experiment involving monkeys that illustrates this very powerfully. Scientists put several monkeys into a large enclosure. In the middle of the enclosure there was a tall wooden pole with a bunch of bananas on the top. When the monkeys tried to reach the bananas they were blasted with a high-pressure water hose. Although it didn't hurt them, it was obviously not an enjoyable experience and eventually all the monkeys stopped trying to get the bananas.

Then they removed one of the original monkeys and added a new monkey to the group. Although accepted by the group, as soon as he spotted the bananas and went to retrieve them all the remaining monkeys pulled him off the pole – even though this time there was no water hose. They had been conditioned to believe that climbing the pole equalled pain so they were 'saving' the new monkey from harm.

Soon even the new monkey stopped trying to climb the pole. Eventually all the original monkeys were replaced one by one until none of the monkeys in the enclosure had witnessed or experienced the actual water treatment and yet none of them would make any attempt to go up the pole and get the bananas.

Like those monkeys, we judge what is acceptable by those around us. If you're in debt and your family and friends are in debt then it can't be that bad – right? Actually, yes it can, but it's very possible that even if you recognise it and try to change it those around you will try to 'pull you off the pole'. This is partly because they don't want to see you fail and partly because they actually don't want to see you succeed either – otherwise they may have to change too. If you make any attempt to alter the status quo you are likely to meet some resistance. Sadly, it is often those who supposedly love us the most who discourage us the most.

HERE'S AN IDEA FOR YOU...

What do those closest to you believe about money? If you don't know, ask. You may be surprised to find out that you are similar in terms of what you make, what you spend and how much you owe. See if they would like to change their situation too and create a Richest Man in Babylon club to support each other.

3 HARD WORK IS NO GUARANTEE OF WEALTH

Bansir laments, *'From early dawn until darkness stopped me, I have labored to build the finest chariots any man could make, softheartedly hoping some day the gods would recognise my worthy deeds and bestow upon me great prosperity. This they have never done. At last, I realise this they will never do.'*

We are all taught in school that if we work hard and get good exam results we'll get a good job and everything will be OK. And maybe in days gone by that idea was valid; certainly the concept of a job for life was common. But it's no longer accurate. Hard work alone is not a ticket to wealth – and it never has been.

Just look at Charles Goodyear. His name is synonymous with his most important innovation – the car tyre. Goodyear developed the process of vulcanisation, turning rubber into a material with limitless possible uses. He was a brilliantly inventive man and pursued his ideas with determination and passion, and yet his

DEFINING IDEA...

When a man tells you he got rich through hard work, ask him 'whose?'
~ DON MARQUIS, AUTHOR

hard work and ingenuity did not make him rich. Indeed, at one point he and his family were living in one of his failed rubber factories on Staten Island eating the fish he caught from the river. Despite the undeniable contribution Goodyear made to the world he never benefited financially. He was, by all accounts, an unlucky chap and was clearly not that good in business yet he remained remarkably philosophical about that fact: 'Life should not be estimated exclusively by the standard of dollars and cents. I am not disposed to complain that I have planted and others have gathered the fruits. A man has cause for regret only when he sows and no one reaps.'

And yet how much you earn is no indication of your potential to accumulate wealth, either. There are lorry drivers and office cleaners who quietly accumulated wealth using the techniques that came out of Babylon more than 8000 years ago. There are also high-flying stockbrokers with million pound bonuses who live so far beyond their means that they are worse than broke, so how much money you make is also irrelevant.

As long as you have an income or a way to make money you have the potential to create wealth. Hard work without consideration for what you do with your earnings is as futile as laziness. You have to be clever about what you do with what you earn – regardless of how much that is. Otherwise you will come to realise, as Bansir did, that you have been working *year after year living slavish lives. Working, working, working! Getting nowhere…'*

The world does not owe us a living. We need to take charge of our money.

HERE'S AN IDEA FOR YOU…

If you're working hard and wondering where it all goes – find out. Look back over the last month and calculate where your salary was spent. There is no point working like a dog if the money you make slips through your hands. First make an estimate of what was spent on different things and then calculate the truth.

4 SEEK WISE ADVICE

Seeing the futility of their position for the first time Kobbi suggests, *'Might we not find out how others acquired gold and do as they do?'* And so the two friends decide to visit their old friend Arkad – the richest man in Babylon. After all, *'it costs nothing to ask wise advice...'*

DEFINING IDEA...

Very few men are wise by their own counsel, or learned by their own teaching. For he that has only taught by himself had a fool for his master.

~ BEN JONSON, DRAMATIST

According to sociologist Dr Morris Massey we go through three major stages of development, which result in who we become as young adults. From birth to seven years old we are in the 'imprint period' – this is a time when we soak up all the information in our environment and adopt traits of our parents or primary carers. Next comes the 'modelling period' and for the next seven years we are looking outside our environment to find role models we can learn from. This is the age when we have superhero posters on our walls and look up to rock legends and people we hope to emulate. From fourteen to twenty-one, we finally go through the 'socialization period' where we start testing the boundaries we have established and work out what 'fits'.

The modelling phase is an extremely important part of our evolution – and yet when we become adults we stop utilising this source of knowledge. In sport the idea of finding a coach, someone who has either helped others achieve what we desire or has achieved that goal themselves, is well accepted, and yet it doesn't translate so readily into building wealth.

When Andrew Carnegie suggested that Napoleon Hill dedicate his life to understanding success and creating a philosophy that others could follow to achieve that result – what did he do? Did he send him to the library? Did he ask him to launch himself into business and see what happened? Did he tell him to work it out himself? No. He gave him mentors so that he could seek their wise advice. Hill was given unprecedented access to some of the most brilliant, powerful and wealthy men of the day so that he could find out from the horse's mouth how they did what they did. He met with over forty prominent players including Henry Ford, Theodore Roosevelt, John D. Rockefeller, Thomas Edison and F. W. Woolworth. With their insight and knowledge Hill was able to synthesise the philosophy for success and write the greatest personal development book ever written – *Think and Grow Rich*.

The fastest way to learn anything is to learn from someone who has already mastered the skill you seek. It may come as a surprise to know that when asked, most people will *'give freely of their wisdom as men of broad experience are always glad to do'*.

HERE'S AN IDEA FOR YOU...

Who do you know in your local community who is wealthy or well off? Most people are flattered if you ask them for advice. Contact them either by letter or through a personal connection and propose you buy them lunch in exchange for some advice on how they became so successful. The ego is a powerful thing...

5 THE JOY OF RESIDUAL INCOME!

"'Income, that is the thing," ejaculated Bansir. *"I wish an income that will keep flowing into my purse whether I sit upon the wall or travel to far lands.'"* Bansir admired that Arkad received income regardless of whether he was working or not and wanted to learn how to do the same.

When it comes to creating wealth, then residual income (which is also known as passive income) is the Holy Grail. We all dream of having a profession or business that generates money regardless of whether we are at the office, in our pyjamas or lying on a beach in Acapulco.

DEFINING IDEA...

It takes as much imagination to create debt as to create income.
~ LEONARD ORR, AUTHOR

Every year we get envious of Noddy Holder and the boys from Slade who have probably made more money from 'So here it is, Merry Christmas' than from the rest of their entire repertoire, and George Michael is probably still making a killing with 'Last Christmas'. Or what about authors like J. K. Rowling and Stephen King, who continue to receive royalties long after they wrote the last word of one of their bestselling books?

So how can you create residual income? According to wealth-creation guru and author Robert Kiyosaki there are essentially only two valid ways: income from investments or income from a business. In his book *The Cashflow Quadrant* Kiyosaki says there are four ways to generate income:

- E – employee
- S – self-employed
- B – business
- I – investments

Kiyosaki says that you're in the worst position as an employee. The government takes its share before you even get your hands on your money, so the amount you have to invest in order to create more wealth is immediately limited. For the self-employed it's often not that much better – especially as many people who decide to work for themselves end up working harder, longer and for less money than they did before.

The fastest way to create financial freedom is by creating a profitable and efficient business that operates both with or without your direct involvement. This is, however, not as easy as that relatively short sentence would seem to imply! And finally, investments are about finding a way to make the money you do make work even harder for you and thus create additional income. But income is the key, making money in the first place is important. That way you can invest some of that income in the future and slowly multiply your savings.

Arkad was the richest man in Babylon because he understood the nature of money and the need to put the money you make – however much that is – to work for you. It was this strategy that made him wealthy. And it's this strategy that you can employ, regardless of whether you work for someone else, for yourself or have your own business.

HERE'S AN IDEA FOR YOU...

Income is key to generating wealth because it gives you a starting point from which to begin multiplying that wealth. Come up with five possible ways that you could make more money. Is there something that you're good at or enjoy doing that could be marketed to the local community? Get creative.

6 YOU GET WHAT YOU FOCUS ON

Kobbi is excited by the prospect of visiting Arkad and asking him for advice on how to accumulate wealth. Insightfully he says, *'Thou bringeth to my mind a new understanding. Thou makest me realise the reason why we have never found any measure of wealth. We have never sought it.'*

Bansir had *'laboured patiently to build the staunchest chariots in Babylon'*; Kobbi had striven *'to become a skilful lyre player'*. Their best efforts were focused on becoming successful in their field, and not in the accumulation of wealth through that ability. This is a common error.

DEFINING IDEA...

Most people have no idea of the giant capacity we can immediately command when we focus all of our resources on mastering a single area of our lives.

~ ANTHONY ROBBINS, SPEAKER AND AUTHOR

In 2004 the Ig Nobel Prize for Psychology – for achievements that 'make you laugh, then think' – went to Daniel Simons of the University of Illinois and Christopher Chabris of Harvard for a fascinating study that illustrated the power of focus. They asked a group of people to watch a video of a game of basketball and during the game they had to make a note of how many passes one side made – they were told what to focus on. During the video someone in a gorilla suit walked onto the court and, for a full seven seconds, wandered amongst the players. At one point the gorilla even turned to the camera and beat its chest. When the viewers were later quizzed about the video clip, less than half of them had spotted the gorilla. Why? Because they were so focused on counting the passes that they didn't see anything else – including the gorilla.

The same occurs in life. We are so busy doing a job and hopefully doing it well that we forget to then turn our focus on the fruits of that labour. Part of the reason for that is that we are never taught to focus on money.

One of the quirks of life is that some of the most important information we need in order to make a success of it is not contained in the school curriculum. We are partly prepared for the world of work in so far as we can count and write and communicate to some degree, but we are not prepared for the results of that work. We are given no guidance about how to manage money and how to accumulate and build wealth to provide for our families and ourselves. There is no focus placed on money management in any part of our formal education. If there were, then accountants would not be in debt.

If you want to change your financial fortunes you have to make it a priority and focus on that outcome. Kobbi reminds us, *'Now at last, we see a light, bright like that from the rising sun. It biddeth us to learn more that we may prosper more.'*

HERE'S AN IDEA FOR YOU...
Make a list of all the things that you have spent time on (either in action or in your thoughts) over the last week. Have a look at where you spend your time and where your focus is directed. Are any of them conducive to accumulating money and becoming financially secure?

7 FICKLE FATE WON'T MAKE YOU RICH

Bansir and Kobbi meet Arkad and are keen to learn the 'secret' that has separated their fortunes. Was it luck? Arkad warns, *"Fickle Fate" is a vicious goddess who brings no permanent good to anyone. On the contrary, she brings ruin to almost every man upon whom she showers unearned gold'.*

DEFINING IDEA...
A fool and his money are soon parted.
~ PROVERB

Like Bansir and Kobbi, we are often desperate to attribute success to factors outside our control. The accumulation of money is not dependent on connections, existing wealth, background, skill, intelligence or any other of the very many 'excuses' we could come up with. It's not even about luck. It is, as Arkad reminds his old friends, *'because you either have failed to learn the laws that govern the building of wealth, or else you do not observe them'.*

When it comes to 'Fickle Fate', just look at lottery winners. Surely that must be good luck? Surely winning an enormous and life-changing sum of money will set the winners on a happy, secure and wealthy path? Apparently not. Although it's hard to establish the true statistics of just how many lottery winners eventually go belly up, the numbers are thought to be high. If you go to an Internet search engine and type in 'lottery winners lose everything' and surf through some of the 178,000 or so websites considered relevant you'll find the same story repeated right across the globe.

It goes something like this. Win millions in the lottery, celebrate, quit your job, buy a string of expensive toys, a mansion (most likely one at home and another one abroad), go on a six-month holiday, flying first class and staying in five-star hotels, give some money to friends and family if they are still speaking to you, get hounded by people you've never met or haven't seen since playgroup – only to wake up one morning a few years later not only broke but millions in debt.

Take the case of John McGuinness, for example. He won £10,055,900 in a £40 million UK lottery rollover in 1996. At the time of his win he was earning just £150 a week and sleeping on his parents' floor after splitting up with his first wife. Bless him, he lavished £3 million on his family and even gave his ex-wife £750,000! He went on to buy a Ferrari Modena Spyder for £140,000 together with five other exclusive cars. He relaxed on a Caribbean cruise and bought a villa in Majorca and spent £200,000 getting married again to wife number two. In February 2008 he was seeking a council house in Scotland and was £2.1 million in debt. And John McGuinness is not an exception.

Arkad reminds us that easy money is actually a false god. *'She makes wanton spenders, who soon dissipate all they receive and are left beset by overwhelming appetites and desires they have not the ability to gratify.'*

HERE'S AN IDEA FOR YOU...

Forget lotteries and instead use the money you would usually waste on tickets to either pay off your debts or accumulate wealth. Yes, you may have to 'be in it to win it', but the vast majority of people don't win any more than an insignificant amount.

8 THE SCROOGE EFFECT

Arkad goes on to warn of Fate, *'Yet others who she favors become misers and hoard their wealth, fearing to spend what they have, knowing they do not possess the ability to replace it. They further are beset by fear of robbers and doom themselves to lives of emptiness and secret misery.'*

DEFINING IDEA...

Be your own palace or the world is your jail.
~ JOHN DONNE

When Lady Luck shines on some they spend their financial windfall and manage to get themselves into a worse position than when they started. It turns others into misers – tortured by the thought of its loss.

The problem with winning money, or even inheriting it, is that the money was not made possible by something the person concerned actually did. Its arrival was outside their control, and should it disappear there is no way for them to replace it.

On the other hand, money accumulated because of conscious activity puts a person firmly in charge of their destiny. There is no fear that something might happen which causes them to lose it, because even if they do lose it they know how to make it again.

Take Gerald Ratner, for example. Joining the family business at fifteen, straight out of school, he went on to revolutionise the retail jewellery industry. Ratner's made £1.2 billion in sales and he was a very wealthy man. Then he made a notorious speech. In 1991, in front of 6000 businesspeople, he joked that Ratner's earrings were 'cheaper than an M&S prawn sandwich but probably wouldn't last as long'. He went on to add, 'We also do cut-glass sherry decanters complete with six glasses on a silver-plated tray that your butler can serve you drinks on, all for £4.95. People say, "How can you sell this for such a low price?" I say, "Because it's total crap".' He received a standing ovation for the speech and he'd made the same jokes many times before – only there had obviously never been any tabloid journalists in the audience on previous occasions. His comments about his own merchandise received widespread publicity.

At the time of the unfortunate remarks Ratner's was the world's largest jewellery retailer with profits in excess of £120 million. Gerald Ratner's gaffe sent shockwaves through the market and wiped an estimated £500 million off the company's share value, and he was eventually forced out of the business. He lost everything. He was fired from the only job he'd ever had and his once good reputation was in tatters.

But Gerald Ratner is a very smart man – despite his flippant comments indicating the opposite. Although he went through a very difficult time, he was eventually able to recreate the wealth he lost. His ability and determination as a businessman was sufficient for it not to matter what 'Fickle Fate' threw at him; he was strong enough, smart enough and capable enough to make a fortune all over again.

HERE'S AN IDEA FOR YOU...

There is a saying, 'If you think education is expensive try ignorance.' If you feel that a lack of education about finance is holding you back, rectify the situation. Find night classes that would give you the basics of accounting and financial management, or go to the local library. Invest some time in learning more.

9 THE FIRST LESSON – PAY YOURSELF FIRST

Arkad told his friends of the first lesson he learnt about wealth. *'A part of all you earn is yours to keep. It should be not less than a tenth no matter how little you earn. It can be as much more as you can afford. Pay yourself first.'*

Arkad goes on to clarify: *'Do not buy from the clothes maker and the sandal maker more than you can pay out of the rest and still have enough for food and charity and penance to the gods.'*

DEFINING IDEA...

The saving man becomes the free man.
– CHINESE PROVERB

The idea is simple – for every £1 you receive in your hand you set aside at least 10p. You remove that 10% and put it in a safe place, away from even rainy-day requirements. Then, and only then, do you pay your bills and spend your earnings on the things you want. This is a reverse of the process that is more normally practised. Instead we spend everything we earn, buy whatever takes our fancy and if we can't really afford it we just borrow at least 10%. Rainy days are forgotten, and there is rarely any left over for savings. Effectively we pay ourselves last, if at all.

This idea of saving 10% is often associated with religious donations where people would tithe a part of their income to a church or temple. 'Tithe' is old English for 'tenth' and was a voluntary contribution to a chosen cause. Whether or not this practice afforded the donors bonus points at the gates of heaven or not is open to conjecture; however, it is a proven method for accumulating wealth (either your own or the church's).

Wealth must be fostered, and that means fostered in the mind as well as in the pocket. The idea of paying yourself first is the fundamental principal of wealth creation that has been regurgitated by every investment guru or money expert since it was first engraved on a clay tablet in Babylon.

Saving teaches us self-discipline. By getting into the routine of saving part of your income you learn to temper your desires – and it also makes you feel better as, little by little, the little turns into a lot. All too often, however, we are seduced by those bright red stilettos from the sandal maker or the latest 'must have' new suit from the clothes maker, and instead we spend all we earn plus a little more.

'Wealth, like a tree, grows from a tiny seed. The first copper you save is the seed from which your tree of wealth shall grow. The sooner you plant that seed the sooner shall the tree grow. And the more faithfully you nourish and water that tree with consistent savings, the sooner may you bask in contentment beneath its shade.'

HERE'S AN IDEA FOR YOU...

Open a special RMIB (Richest Man in Babylon) account and set up a direct debit from the account that receives your pay to the new savings account. Automatically move 10% of what you earn every month. If you do not make the same every month, deposit 10% manually. Do not touch the money in your RMIB account under any circumstances.

10 SEEK WISE ADVICE – FROM THE RIGHT PEOPLE!

"'Every fool must learn," he growled, "but why trust the knowledge of a brick maker about jewels? Would you go to the bread maker to enquire about the stars? No, by my tunic you would go to the astrologer, if you had then power to think. Your savings are gone…"'

DEFINING IDEA...

Never trust the advice of a man in difficulties.
~ AESOP

Just as Bansir and Kobbi sought out wise advice from Arkad, he once sought that same advice from a wealthy money lender called Algamish. Arkad had faithfully followed his mentor's advice and saved 10% of all he earned. But in finding a good home for those savings he had trusted the advice of someone who was not an expert and had lost it all.

If you want to create wealth you have to be careful who you take advice from. All too often we share our dreams with our friends and family members only to be shot down in flames. We allow the opinion of others to influence our decisions far too easily and take advice from people totally unqualified to give it. Arkad learned the hard way by trusting that a brick maker would be able to source good jewels. But the man knew nothing about jewels and so, even with the best intentions, Arkad's savings were doomed.

Getting the right advice is essential, and being prepared to pay a little more for the best is worth it.

I remember when I was living in Sydney and had been writing professionally for about a year. I visited my usual accountant to prepare my tax return and the estimate of my tax bill made my eyes water! I decided I should try and get a second opinion and a friend who was also a writer recommended her accountant, who was used to working with writers and might possibly have some better advice. I made an appointment and showed him the draft return. It took him less than five seconds to spot the error. Writing is one of the few professions that allows you to average out your income over a number of years to account for the inevitable fluctuations. My old accountant had not known this or, if he had, he had not remembered to apply it to me. Although my new accountant charged 25% more for his services he was able to legitimately reduce my tax liability by over 60%.

Information is priceless – you don't have time to master every skill and area of expertise you need to create wealth so you have to trust someone in the end. A good professional saves you time and makes you money and will also educate you along the way.

The warning is simple, and well worth heeding. *'Advice is one thing that is freely given away. But watch that you take only what is worth having.'*

HERE'S AN IDEA FOR YOU…

When you need advice on something stop and think about who is best placed to give you that advice. You wouldn't ask your three-times divorced friend for advice on relationships, so why take financial advice from people in a worse or similar position to you? If you don't know anyone then find a good professional and pay for it.

11 DEFINITENESS OF PURPOSE

'For four years did I not prove my definiteness of purpose...? Would you call a fisherman lucky who for years so studied the habits of the fish that with changing wind he could cast his nets about them? Opportunity is a haughty goddess who wastes no time with those that are unprepared.'

DEFINING IDEA...
Winners are people with definite purpose in life.
~ DENIS WAITLEY, SPEAKER AND AUTHOR

It's easy to look at those people who have succeeded and assume that they just got lucky. But, invariably, behind the façade of 'overnight success' is an unwavering commitment and definiteness of purpose that makes successful people able to do whatever needs to be done in order to achieve their goal of financial prosperity.

When it comes to unwavering commitment, George Sampson is a name that may not spring immediately to mind. At the time of writing, he was a fourteen-year-old street dancer from the city of Manchester competing in the TV talent show *Britain's Got Talent*. What makes him so special is that he entered the competition in 2007 and was put out before the semi-finals. But he never gave up; he took the criticism he received on board and applied again in 2008, by which time he was five inches taller and more determined than ever to fulfil his dream. He dances in the street to raise money for lessons and practises for at least four hours every day. His performance in the final was phenomenal and he won the contest against stiff competition. Opportunity may be a haughty goddess, but she shone on George Sampson simply because he was so prepared. He gave the performance of his young life and deserves every possible success.

Whether your dream is to become a famous dancer or to become free of financial worries, you must set that goal as your definite major purpose and refuse to allow anything to pull you from that course.

To reinforce the point, consider this. In his book *As A Man Thinketh* James Allen says, 'They who have no central purpose in their life fall an easy prey to petty worries, fears, troubles, and self-pitying, all of which lead, just as surely as deliberately planned sins to failure, unhappiness, and loss. A man should conceive of a legitimate purpose in his heart, and set out to accomplish it. He should make this purpose his supreme duty, and should devote himself to its attainment, not allowing his thoughts to wander away into ephemeral fancies, longings, and imaginings.'

Erratic action toward your goal will produce an erratic result. Arkad reminds us that, *'Will power is but the unflinching purpose to carry a task you set for yourself to fulfilment. If I set for myself a task, be it ever so trifling, I shall see it through. How else shall I have confidence in myself to do important things?'*

HERE'S AN IDEA FOR YOU...

What is it that you most want to achieve? If you're reading this, then I'm guessing that you want to make more money or get yourself out of debt. Whatever it is, decide your goal and remind yourself of it every day as soon as you wake up. Make everything you do lead to that outcome.

12 DISCIPLINE AND CONSISTENCY ARE KEY

'For a hundred days… I pick a pebble and cast it into the stream. If on the seventh day I passed by without remembering, I would not say to myself "Tomorrow I will cast two pebbles which will do as well". Instead, I would retrace my steps and cast the pebble.'

Here Arkad is stressing the importance of consistent disciplined action when it comes to achieving the goals we set in life – especially building wealth. If you resolve to improve your financial position and adopt the habit of saving one-tenth of all you make, all your good work is ruined as soon as you dip into those funds, invest unwisely or simply choose to break the rule.

Arkad goes on to say, *'Nor on the twentieth day would I say to myself, "Arkad, this is useless. What does it avail you to cast a pebble every day? Throw in a handful and be done with it." No, I would not say that nor do it. When I set a task for myself, I complete it.'*

It is this discipline to consistently do what you set your mind to do that separates success from failure. Curiously, few people recognise the inextricable link that exists between lack of discipline and failure. Most people see failure as being one earth-shattering event, such as a company going bankrupt or a house being repossessed. But, as Jim Rohn points out in his book *Seven Strategies for Wealth and Happiness*, this is not how failure happens: 'Failure is rarely the result of some isolated event. Rather it is a consequence of a long list of accumulated little failures, which happen as a result of too little discipline.'

The power of consistent action and disciplined effort can clearly be seen in another vitally important area – health. Gym membership databases the world over are bulging with the details of Lycra-primed members with good intentions but little else. Following the Christmas blowout our aspirations of five workouts a week dwindle to once (if we're lucky) during which we 'throw a handful in and be done with it' by almost killing ourselves on the treadmill. Yet all the best advice says that short, frequent and consistent exercise is much healthier than sporadic bursts. So thirty minutes on a regular basis is infinitely more beneficial than one and a half hours of hell…

If you've ever managed to reach the dizzy heights of 'fit' you'll also know just how quickly that fitness is lost when you decide to take a few nights off. Health, like wealth, is something that is built over time. It doesn't happen overnight and it demands consistent effort. Clason reminds us through Arkad's story that, *'Wealth grows, wherever men exert energy.'*

HERE'S AN IDEA FOR YOU...

Look at your credit card statements for the past six months. Are they a 'long list of accumulated little failures which happen as a result of too little discipline' – the unused gadget you 'had' to have or the shoes you never wear? Was your life enriched by the purchase? No? Then you may need to get reacquainted with discipline.

13 IF IT'S TOO GOOD TO BE TRUE IT PROBABLY IS

Once savings have been accrued you must, *'learn to make your treasure work for you. Make its children and its children's children work for you.'* **But be warned,** *'Usurious rates of return are deceitful sirens that sing but to lure the unwary upon the rocks of lose and remorse.'*

Speaking of 'rocks of lose and remorse', for most Britons the news that Northern Rock, the UK's fifth largest mortgage provider, was in trouble in September 2007 was the first they knew of the term 'sub-prime' – or of its ramifications.

DEFINING IDEA...

As house prices fall, a huge amount of financial folly is being exposed. You only learn who has been swimming naked when the tide goes out – and what we are witnessing at some of our largest financial institutions is an ugly sight.

~ WARREN BUFFETT

Northern Rock sought emergency funding from the Bank of England because inter-bank lending had dried up as global finance braced itself for the fallout of the US sub-prime lending problem (a market Northern Rock was itself heavily involved in). Traditionally, mortgages were funded from customer deposits. This, of course, limited the number of people banks could lend to. So some bright spark in the US came up with the idea of bundling the debt into complex financial derivatives and selling it on to other financial institutions at a reduced interest rate. They might charge borrowers 6.5% and then sell that debt with 5.5% interest – making 1% profit. This allowed them to take a profit, sell unlimited mortgages and offset the risk!

It wasn't long before lending criteria and assessment virtually disappeared, and as long as a borrower had a pulse they could get a mortgage. This was known as the sub-prime market and was very lucrative indeed. The brokers didn't care if their clients could pay because they got their commission regardless; the banks didn't really care either because they were making 'usurious' profits and were happy to ignore the inevitable rocks on the horizon. Besides property was booming, so the asset was worth more than the debt anyway…

Happy days!

Then the bottom fell out the housing market and the loan default rate rocketed. If you think of sub-prime loans (not the people!) as being like a rotten apple, then rather than throw the rotten apple away – by refusing the loan – the banks cut it into little bits and packaged it with good apples. Eventually, however, there was so much rotten apple in the system that nothing could hide it. The world's banks battened down the hatches and stopped lending to each other – which was what caused Northern Rock's problems – and braced themselves for a correction. In April 2008 the International Monetary Fund (IMF) put the cost of that rotten apple at $565 billion, with aggregate potential losses to about $945 billion dollars. That's a lot of rotten apple…

So perhaps it's time we all heed the advice of ancient Babylon and realise that, *'A small return and a safe one is far more desirable than risk.'*

HERE'S AN IDEA FOR YOU…

If you can't raise a deposit to buy the home you want, rent. Save the difference between what your mortgage repayments would have been and the rent you actually pay. That way, you get to feel what it's like to pay a mortgage – and save for your deposit at the same time.

14 PAY FAIR TAXES

"'Why should so few men be able to acquire all the gold?"
"Because they know how," replied the Chancellor. "One may
not condemn a man for succeeding because he knows how.
Neither may one with justice take away from a man what he
has fairly earned, to give to men of less ability.'"

DEFINING IDEA...
In this world nothing is
certain but death and taxes.
~ BENJAMIN FRANKLIN

In the third chapter of *The Richest Man in Babylon*, Clason discusses the 'Seven Cures for a Lean Purse'. The King is concerned about the uneven distribution of wealth occurring in Babylon. In 8000 years this concern hasn't changed much, as commentators continue to suggest that 'the rich get richer and the poor get poorer'.

The challenge that faces every government is how to distribute wealth. On one hand you have people who are wealthy, who can afford the best accountants, solicitors and lawyers that money can buy. They hire people who understand the system (and the loopholes) and consequently they manage their tax liability inventively, albeit legally.

Take British high-street retailer Sir Philip Green, for example. His family is reported to be worth £4.9 billion. In 2005 his businesses generated £1.2 billion in dividends and yet he didn't pay any income tax. His wife owns most of his business, and she lives in Monaco and – lo and behold – Monaco doesn't impose a tax on dividends. People like Sir Philip probably feel justified in protecting their wealth for the reasons the Chancellor explained to the King in Babylon. Some of the super-rich probably work very hard and they do provide jobs for thousands of others.

But is it fair? Conversely, is it fair that decent, hard-working people are taxed to within an inch of their lives? They are taxed before they even get their income, with few possibilities for creative accountancy. The rich don't subsidise the poor; it's the other way around.

Perhaps it should no longer be about the 'haves and the have nots' but about the 'trys and the try nots'. Why should either the rich or the hard-working, struggling family subsidise those individuals who have no intention of ever getting a job because the benefits they receive far outstrip any job they could get? What sort of stupidity penalises those who genuinely want to work but can't because they can't afford to? Even doing a few hours a week would slash their benefits and make survival difficult as a result. Is it right that either group should support people who make no effort to better their position whatsoever?

We all need to pay tax, but the tax systems in many countries need an overhaul to encourage those who have 'fairly earned' their money through hard work and commitment to take care of their family and support those who genuinely are unable to do so. The rest should get a move on and do something useful.

HERE'S AN IDEA FOR YOU...

It's been estimated that 5.7 million UK taxpayers might not be paying the right tax. If you're an employee and pay through PAYE, check your code (around £500 million may have been overpaid because of code errors). It's on your pay slip – check online that it reflects your current situation. Contact the tax office if it doesn't.

15 START THY PURSE TO FATTENING

"Arkad," continued the King, "our city is in a very unhappy state because a few men know how to acquire wealth and therefore monopolize it, while the mass of our citizens lack the knowledge of how to keep any part of the gold they receive."

DEFINING IDEA...

The habit of saving is itself an education. It fosters every virtue, teaches self-denial, cultivates the sense of order, trains to forethought, and so broadens the mind.

~ THORNTON T. MUNGER, US SCIENTIST

Each night, for seven nights Arkad was asked to teach a class of 100 men the cures for a lean purse. The first cure? *'For every ten coins thou placest within thy purse take out for use but nine. Thy purse will start to fatten at once and its increasing weight will feel good in thy hand and bring satisfaction to thy soul.'*

Its relevance is even more important today when you consider these figures for the UK as an example:

- Total personal debt at the end of December 2007 stood at £1409 billion.
- Total consumer credit lending to individuals in December 2007 was £224 billion.
- Average household debt is £8985 (excluding mortgages). This figure increases to £20,895 if the average is based on the number of households who actually have some form of unsecured loan.
- Personal debt is increasing by £1 million every five minutes.
- In an average day 24.5 million transactions worth £1.4 billion will be

spent on plastic cards. Consumers will borrow an additional £327 million and will pay £259 million in interest for the privilege…

According to uSwitch, Britain is suffering from a bad case of affluenza: '…We are caught in the grip of a spiral of conspicuous consumption where it's no longer enough to keep up with the Joneses, but instead we want to live like our favourite celebrities; 4.8 million adults spend more than they earn and 9 million adults just break even at the end of every month.'

It would seem that for every ten coins we place in the purse we take out ten or even eleven. So our purse doesn't fatten leading to worry and sleepless nights. Is it really worth it? *'Which desirest thou the most? Is it the gratification of thy desires of each day, a jewel, a bit of finery, better raiment, more food; things quickly gone and forgotten? Or is it substantial belongings, gold, lands, herds, merchandise, income-bringing investments? The coins thou takest from thy purse bring the first. The coins thou leavest within it will bring the latter.'*

If we are ever to experience financial freedom we must rid ourselves of bad debt (debt that is not asset related) and religiously set aside at least 10% of all we make. Arkad warns us, *'Deride not what I say because of its simplicity. Truth is always simple.'*

HERE'S AN IDEA FOR YOU...
The only way to successfully use credit cards is to pay off the balance each month, but only 58% of credit card holders do so. If you don't, go to your wallet right now and cut up at least one card. In the UK alone there are more credit cards than people, so we could all do to downsize.

16 CONTROL EXPENDITURE

The second cure for a lean purse is, *'Budget thy expenses that thou mayest have coins to pay for thy necessities, to pay for thy enjoyments and to gratify thy worthwhile desires without spending more than nine-tenths of thy income.'* Budgeting is often viewed as limiting, but it can be liberating.

Arkad tells his students, *'Now I will tell thee an unusual truth about men and sons of men. It is this; that what each of us calls our "necessary expenses" will always grow to equal our incomes unless we protest to the contrary. Confuse not the necessary expenses with thy desires.'*

DEFINING IDEA...

Beware of little expenses. A small leak will sink a great ship.

~ BENJAMIN FRANKLIN

Brendan Nichols is an international speaker and author on the subject of generating more money from your business. He refers to this phenomenon as the 'looking good, going nowhere syndrome'.

You can see this syndrome playing itself out in corporate offices up and down the land, in every country, and it is often manifest in what is known as 'golden handcuffs'. Traditionally this is a system of financial incentives that makes it very difficult for an employee to leave a company. It may take the form of stock options that will not mature for several years, or perhaps there is a contractual obligation to repay bonuses should the recipient leave. But there is also a much more insidious force at work. As someone climbs the corporate ladder, more often than not, their salary will climb with them. Soon, as Arkad warns, their necessary expenses grow equal to their incomes (if not beyond). They trade up to the large detached house with the big garden, smart designer outfits and accessories replace high-street shopping and the comfortable family saloon is exchanged for a BMW. As a result, many people become chained to jobs they hate because they need their inflated salary to service their inflated expenses. The 'trappings' of wealth are well named.

You have to differentiate between your needs and your wants. First, you have to work out what your 'must money' is – this is the absolute minimum you need in order to meet your commitments and survive. After that you need to prioritise your desires and *'Budget then thy necessary expenses'.*

Many people shy away from budgeting because it implies constraint, and yet it delivers exactly the opposite – freedom. *'The purpose of a budget is to help thy purse to fatten. It is to assist thee to have thy necessities and, insofar as attainable, thy other desires. It is to enable thee to realize thy most cherished desires by defending them from thy casual wishes. Like a bright light in a dark cave thy budget shows up the leaks from thy purse and enables thee to stop them and control thy expenditures for definite and gratifying purposes.'*

HERE'S AN IDEA FOR YOU...

Keep a money journal for seven days. Make a note of what and how much you spend – and no cheating! Calculate the total and look for the 'leaks from thy purse'. You may be surprised to find that 'certain accepted expenses may wisely be reduced or eliminated' – for example, apparently a third of all groceries end up in the dustbin.

17 NO ONE CAN HAVE EVERYTHING THEY WANT!

Arkad tells his students, *'All men are burdened with more desires than they can gratify. Because of my wealth thinkest thou I may gratify every desire? 'Tis a false idea. There are limits to my time... my strength... to the distance I may travel... and to the zest with which I may enjoy.'*

This is a valid point and one that is easily lost when we are seeking a better financial position. We dream of wealth and all the wonderful things we will do, buy and have when we finally manage to turn our financial fortunes around. But even the very wealthy have constraints on what they are able to do.

DEFINING IDEA...

If we get everything that we want, we soon want nothing that we get.
~ VERNON LUCHIES, MINISTER

Do you honestly think Bill Gates can spend his time and money exactly as he wants? Is it not more likely that he has a team of people who require him to account for everything – including his time and money? I doubt very much that Bill Gates could or would throw a sickie and go fishing, for example, if he felt the need for a 'mental health day'. Or what about Warren Buffett, the 'Oracle of Omaha', who in 2008 knocked Bill Gates off the top of the Forbes Rich List and is now the world's wealthiest individual? Do you think he has the freedom to do as he pleases or would the stock of Berkshire Hathaway tumble if he were to take a sickie? Consider – extreme wealth usually brings with it extreme responsibility. And while limits may not exist on what the super-rich can buy, we all have only twenty-four hours in a day.

Considering that 70% of British adults play the national lottery on a regular basis and the weekly sales of lottery-related products is around £100 million every single week, it's safe to assume that most people want 'more money'. The great news is that you don't actually need to be rich in financial terms to have a good life. In fact 'rich' can be a nightmare – just ask some of those jackpot winners. If you are going to turn your financial situation around, then you have to start saving, clear your debts and learn where your money goes so you can stem the flow of wasted cash.

Write out all the things that you desire to buy right now – even the whacky ones. Then *'select those that are necessary and others that are possible through the expenditure of nine tenths of thy income. Cross out the rest and consider them but a part of that great multitude of desires that must go unsatisfied and regret them not.'*

So forget Learjets and diamonds. Forget owning a football club (that's what sunk John McGuinness in Idea 7). Forget racehorses and Maseratis… at least for now.

HERE'S AN IDEA FOR YOU…

How much would 'enough' be? Make a list of all the things you'd like if you had money. Score off the ridiculous ones and attribute a figure to the ones that really matter, such as paying off your debts and your mortgage. Total up your dream life – you may be surprised to discover that you don't need millions.

18 MAKE MONEY MULTIPLY

The third cure for a lean purse is, *'to put each coin to laboring that it may reproduce its kind even as the flocks of the field and help bring to thee income, a stream of wealth that shall flow constantly into thy purse.'*

DEFINING IDEA...

It's not the bulls and the bears you need to avoid – it's the bum steers.

~ CHUCK HILLIS, US BUSINESSMAN

Of all Arkad's wisdom, this is perhaps the insight that belies the greatest complexity. Arkad learnt his lesson because he trusted his life savings to a brick maker who was swindled with *'worthless bits of glass'* because he knew nothing about jewels.

Making shrewd investments is probably more complicated today because the brick makers are far more adept at pretending to be jewellers…

So how do you find good, honourable investments that will both look after your money and add to your wealth?

If you're already a millionaire then it's certainly a lot easier. You could go on the panel of the TV show Dragons' Den, for example, where hundreds of budding inventors and entrepreneurs present their varied cases. Granted, you'd have to listen to countless passionate but deluded ideas, such an underwater theme park, but every now and again you'd find a cracker – an idea so good that you wouldn't need to be a professional businessperson to recognise its sheer brilliance. Take the Reverse Osmosis Sanitation System (ROSS), for example, developed by James Brown and Amanda Jones. This innovative water transport, sanitation and storage device was designed to bring relief to the millions of people across the world without access to safe water. What was so unusual about this particular investment was that all the Dragons invested and they didn't demand more than the 10% equity offered. Normally investors such as the Dragons demand far more equity in a business for the experience, connections and cash they bring.

Where you invest your money depends on a) how much you have and b) your attitude to risk. Arkad warns about seeking ambitious returns as it will invariably lead to loss – however, there are plenty of options to explore. Business angel networks and private equity firms offer a way to invest in Dragons' Den-type opportunities.

The need for good professional advice applies even more strongly if you are tempted to invest in something connected to your family or friends. Remember there is far more at stake than just your money in this sort of situation. Unmet expectations or changes in circumstance can put a huge strain on a relationship – and possibly even end it.

Arkad's first profitable investment was a loan to a man named Aggar, a shield maker. *'Gaining wisdom… I extended my loans and investments as my capital increased. From a few sources at first, from many sources later, flowed into my purse a golden stream of wealth.'* You must do the same.

HERE'S AN IDEA FOR YOU...

Once you have accumulated savings, you need to find a home for that money so it will grow exponentially. Find someone you know who has good investments and ask for advice, or seek a recommendation for a professional advisor. Ask for references and check them thoroughly. Be prepared to pay; 'free' advice can be very expensive.

19 NEW WAYS TO MAKE MONEY MULTIPLY

'I tell you, my students, a man's wealth is not in the coins he carries in his purse; it is the income he buildeth, the golden stream that continually floweth into his purse and keepeth it always bulging. That is what every man desireth.' **Getting money to multiply is the goal.**

In Babylon the options for investments were probably limited to shield makers, chariot makers and brickies masquerading as jewellers. Today the options are endless, and that is not always a good thing.

So if you don't have tens of thousands squirrelled away how do you *'buildeth your income'*? According to online money guru Martin Lewis, anyone who is currently a UK taxpayer should have an Individual Savings Accounts (ISA). ISAs allow you to keep the interest accrued on your savings instead of having to pay tax on it. Remember, it's not always about how much you make; it's about how much you keep!

There are also a plethora of managed funds and unit trusts that offer a lower access point and allow you to invest in a spread of different investments such as property, shares, bonds and cash. Your money is pooled with that of other investors and you can choose funds depending on your risk tolerance. For safer stock market investments there are funds that only invest in blue-chip companies, for example.

But be warned – investments linked to the stock market, even blue-chip ones, can go down as well as up. Projected profit is no guarantee, as many endowment policy holders are finding out… Endowment mortgages were popular in the UK in the 1980s and 90s. It seemed plausible. You paid the lender the interest on the loan only, and then invested an additional payment into an endowment policy, which also provided you – the homebuyer – with life insurance. The endowment was linked to the stock market and the idea was that once the loan term was complete, usually 20–25 years, there would be enough cash in the endowment to pay off the mortgage and possibly provide a nice little nest egg to boot. But the share market is a volatile creature, and by 2003 the government estimated that eight out of every ten active endowments would not pay off the mortgage concerned, never mind provide a bonus on top. Since then, nearly 70% of those facing a shortfall have re-mortgaged, sought financial advice or applied for compensation. However, according to the Financial Services Authority (FSA), that still leaves about 700,000 people who are in for a nasty surprise!

It's important that you realise that many of the 'advisors' out there are nothing more than order takers. Their genuine understanding and knowledge can be quite limited. Get good advice to ensure *'the golden stream continually floweth'.*

HERE'S AN IDEA FOR YOU…

When seeking financial advice ask brokers what policies they have. Ask, 'Would you recommend that your mother invest in this fund?' Providing they like their mother, the instinctive hesitation they might display will be enough of a warning for you to investigate further. Do your homework on past performance.

20 THE MIRACLE OF COMPOUND INTEREST

When it comes to making money multiply, Arkad reminds us of the other powerful way to make money grow: *'The money lender explained that because this sum had been increased by compound interest, the original ten pieces of silver had now grown to thirty and one half pieces.'*

Arkad tells the story of a farmer who took ten pieces of silver to a moneylender when his first son was born and asked him to keep it on rental for his son until he reached the age of twenty.

The farmer knew that time would work its magic on that initial investment through compound interest. Compound interest is the concept of adding accumulated interest back to the principal investment so that future interest is earned on ever-increasing amounts. Time is what makes compound interest work.

DEFINING IDEA...

Hare always reminded himself, 'Don't brag about your lightning pace, for slow and steady won the race!'

~ AESOP, THE TORTOISE AND THE HARE

The Rule of 72 is a very simple way of working out how long it will take for your investment to double in value. Say, for example, you invested $10,000 in a mutual fund paying 12% interest. According to the Rule of 72 it would take six years to become $20,000 (72 divided by 12 is 6). And it would continue to double every six years, meaning your initial $10,000 would be worth $1,280,000 in forty-two years. The Rule of 72 doesn't take taxes, fees or other costs into consideration but it does offer an approximation of the time needed for an investment to double in value – without any further investment on your behalf.

There is no better time to start building wealth than right now. No one plans to be poor, and yet without forward planning many people are. In 2008 over 2.5 million older people in the UK stay in just one heated room of their home to save on heating costs. Over one million older people cut back on food shopping in order to pay for those costs. According to figures provided by Alliance Trust, Britain's pension gap continues to increase with more than a quarter (26%) of British adults failing to make any provision for retirement. Research from Scottish Widows reveals that over 1.5 million of those aged fifty-five and over (34% of that group) claim they can't afford to retire at state retirement age due to a lack of pension savings. Don't become a statistic.

As for the farmer's son, he didn't need the money when he was twenty, so he let it accrue. *'When the son became fifty years of age, the father meantime having passed to the other world, the money lender paid the son in settlement one hundred and sixty-seven pieces of silver. Thus in fifty years had the investment multiplied itself at rental almost seventeen times.'* That is the magic of compound interest.

HERE'S AN IDEA FOR YOU...

If you don't have buckets of money, let compound interest help. If you have children, set up a high-interest bank account in their name and deposit a lump sum. If your child receives money for birthdays, put it in too. Find one that compounds more than once a year and watch it grow. Don't dip into it.

21 GUARD AGAINST LOSS

Arkad warns, *'Misfortune loves a shining mark'* and suggests, therefore, that the fourth cure for a lean purse is to, *'Guard thy treasure from loss by investing only where thy principal is safe, where it may be reclaimed if desirable, and where thou will not fail to collect a fair rental.'*

On the fourth day of teaching, Arkad tells his students that, *'Gold in a man's purse must be guarded with firmness, else it be lost. Thus it is wise that we must first secure small amounts and learn to protect them before the gods entrust us with larger.'*

DEFINING IDEA...

My main philosophy is that my money is a loan from God. I'm in charge of it. I'm responsible for investing it, giving some of it away, providing for my family and protecting it.

~ OREL HERSBIRER, PREACHER

For most people, putting money in a bank is considered safe. They assume that the pitiful interest rates on everyday accounts are a necessary trade-off for that security. But do you really know how safe it is? In the wake of the sub-prime meltdown that shook the global banking sector to the core in 2007–8 there were genuine concerns that one of the top tier banks wouldn't survive. The UK's Northern Rock was taken into public ownership in 2008 and at the time of writing the global financial markets are far from hunky-dory...

If there is a high profile casualty around the corner then you'd better know the rules. Currently the Financial Services Compensation Scheme protects you in the UK – but don't get too excited just yet. It will secure 100% of your deposits up to £2000 and 90% of the next £33,000. The reasonably good news, therefore, is that if you have £35,000 in an institution that got into trouble you would get £31,700 back. The bad news is that if you had £135,000 in that institution you'd still get £31,700 back.

In addition, this compensation only applies to one person per institution so if you've got buckets of cash you need to put smaller eggs in several baskets. Each deposit should be £35,000 or less and the institutions you choose should not be connected to each other. For the sake of compensation, subsidiaries of a parent company count as one institution so, for example, if you had £35,000 in Bank of Scotland and £35,000 with the Halifax you'd only get one payment of £31,700 as compensation because they belong to the same trading group. Wherever you are and however much money you have, do some research before deciding where your savings go.

Developing your wealth is often more about what you keep than what you make, so once you've worked hard to save or earn it you don't want to lose it. You need to seek investments that promise reasonable returns with minimal or no risk to the principal. Arkad closes the lesson by reminding us to, *'Consult with wise men. Secure the advice of those experienced in the profitable handling of gold. Let their wisdom protect thy treasure from unsafe investments.'*

HERE'S AN IDEA FOR YOU...

Find out, for all the places where you have money invested, what would happen if they went belly up. If you don't already know the risk you are carrying, then it's best to find out now while there is still time to minimise it.

22 INVEST IN PLAUSIBLE PROJECTS

When it comes to guarding your money, Arkad warns *'Every owner of gold is tempted by opportunities whereby it would seem that he could make large sums by its investment in most plausible projects.'* **Clason repeats this advice many times throughout his fables, so it's obviously a very important point.**

DEFINING IDEA...

To hazard much to get much has more avarice than wisdom.

~ WILLIAM PENN

I'm not sure if these would constitute entirely 'plausible projects' but one of my personal favourites is the Nigerian email scam, also known as the 419 or 'advanced fee' fraud. These scams don't always come from Nigeria, but they have been emptying the pockets, and the bank accounts, of the gullible for decades.

The 419 scam originated in the early 1980s as the oil-based Nigerian economy declined. Several unemployed university students first used this particular scam as a means of manipulating business visitors interested in shady deals in the Nigerian oil sector before moving on to target businessmen in the west, and later the wider population. The concept is simple. An email is sent from some plausible person – either impersonated or fake – who apparently has millions in various bank accounts but can't get the money out of the country. If the victim helps the person to move the money, they will get a hefty slice of the action. Needless to say there are up-front transaction fees. Incredibly, police estimate that US citizens alone are conned out of some $200 million in this way every year!

And the UK doesn't fare much better. A report conducted in 2006 indicated that fraud of this type cost the UK economy £150m a year – with the average victim losing £31,000. Although the number of people involved is 'vague' (it can't be something you shout about), the sums of money 'have almost certainly run into billions of pounds over the past ten years'.

Other popular cons include pyramid schemes such as the aeroplane system. Initially you pay a fee to become a passenger on the plane and then you need to recruit more passengers so that you move up the pyramid to 'flight crew' then 'co-pilot' and finally 'pilot' – where you supposedly exit the plane with wads of cash. But there is no product changing hands; it's all about the recruitment. Needless to say over 96% of the people who get involved in pyramid schemes never recoup their initial investment.

When it comes to offers of huge profit for little effort, everyone would do well to remember Arkad's advice: *'The first sound principle of investment is security for thy principal. Is it wise to be intrigued by larger earnings when thy principal may be lost? I say not. The penalty of risk is probable loss. Study carefully, before parting with thy treasure, each assurance that it may be safely reclaimed. Be not misled by thine own romantic desires to make wealth rapidly.'*

HERE'S AN IDEA FOR YOU...

You could join the scam-baiters... One responded to the Nigerian scam as 'Father Hector Barnett' of the Church of the Painted Breast! After several emails he informed the sender that he couldn't help because of the death of his friend Minnie Mowse. On second thoughts, don't – these are serious criminals. Just delete the email.

23 CLUES TO A BAD INVESTMENT

One of the clues Arkad offers to test the validity of an investment is the person who is asking you to make it. The warning signs are clearly there when, *'Often friends and relatives are eagerly entering such investment and urge [you] to follow.'* **Beware enthusiastic acquaintances offering financial advice!**

DEFINING IDEA...

Friendship will not stand the strain of very much good advice for very long.

~ ROBERT LYND, WRITER

When it comes to eager friends and relatives urging us to follow, there can be no substitute for network marketing. Many of the big guns are extremely well-run, profitable businesses with excellent products and certainly there are people who have made a success of network marketing – but even the network marking industry acknowledges that the statistics aren't good. Most network marketers sponsor less than three people. Of these, 75% drop out within three months and 95% drop out within a year.

Network marketing may indeed offer a way to supplement your income, but when everyone within a fifty-mile radius who has a pulse is a potential sale you need to have the hide of a rhinoceros to cope with the rejection you must get on a near constant basis. Let's face it, nothing in the known universe can clear a room faster than the arrival of an overzealous Amway representative.

The other disaster waiting to happen is the trap of the stock market 'hot tip'. Successful trader and stock market educator David Novac talks of his evolution as a trader, from novice to professional. His introduction to the stock market came when a colleague enthusiastically urged him to invest in a speculative gold-mining company. At the time the shares were worth 50 cents but were sure to 'go through the roof' and reach $5 a share. With dollar signs in his eyes, David invested his life savings. What followed was an emotional roller-coaster. First there was euphoria as the shares hit $2, but he didn't sell any to recover even part of his investment. Soon panic and regret followed, culminating in despair as the company went into liquidation. He lost everything.

It was a painful and expensive lesson, but it was also one that Novac never forgot. After vowing never to return to the market again, he eventually did get involved once more and this time became very successful at understanding the market and helping others to do the same. But he remains resolute – never trust tips, hot or otherwise.

Arkad, the 'Richest Man in Babylon', lost all his money once because he trusted the advice of someone who knew nothing about the investment concerned. The same applies to eager family members with money glittering in their eyes. Having said that, by the time you've been in a network-marketing organisation for a few months it's highly likely your friends and relatives won't even be eager to speak to you, never mind offer you investment advice!

HERE'S AN IDEA FOR YOU...

Want to make a decision but can't choose? Play stone, paper, scissors. Using chance like this is common in Japan. When Takashi Hashiyama, president of Maspro Denkoh Corporation, wanted to sell their art collection, he needed to decide whether Christie's or Sotheby's got the business. He made them play stone, paper, scissors. Scissors won.

24 OWN YOUR OWN HOME

Arkad says that the fifth cure for a lean purse is to, *'Own thy own home. Thus come many blessings to the man who owneth his own house. And greatly will it reduce his cost of living, making available more of his earnings for pleasures and the gratification of his desires.'*

What Arkad says is still very true, and certainly owning your own home without a mortgage can significantly reduce your cost of living. Unfortunately, however, home ownership is not the panacea it was once considered to be.

In the early 1990s if you wanted to buy a house in the UK you would have been able to borrow between three and three-and-a-half times your gross salary. If you were in a relationship you could either borrow three-and-a-half times the higher salary and one times the other, or three times your joint income. So, for example, if you were single and made £20,000 the most anyone would lend you was £70,000 and to get that you'd have to put down a significant deposit. If you were in a relationship and one of you earned £20,000 and the other earned £18,000, then the most you could borrow would be £114,000.

In March 2007 the average house price across the UK was £194,400. The average national gross salary was £23,600 – less than an eighth of the average cost of a home. Clearly there was a gap.

According to banks and mortgage brokers, the traditional system was 'old hat'. Britain's second biggest mortgage lender, Abbey, changed its rules to allow homebuyers to borrow up to five times their salary; other banks and building societies went further still, offering up to six times their salary. It can be no coincidence that one of those organisations was Northern Rock. At the time of writing it is still under government control after its sub-prime borrowing strategy brought it to its knees.

According to a statement issued well before that happened, Northern Rock said, 'We are encouraging high-quality, low-risk borrowers. As a result of more sophisticated credit assessment we can be more flexible to the specific circumstances of borrowers.' Clearly that didn't pan out – perhaps if they'd paid a little less attention to their 'sophisticated' assessments and applied a dash of common sense the taxpayer wouldn't now be picking up the pieces.

But, to be fair, it wasn't just Northern Rock. Lenders across the board emphatically denied that their actions might prove irresponsible. Oops!

Arkad may be right when he tells his students that, *'no man's family can fully enjoy life unless they do have a plot of ground wherein children can play in the clean earth and where the wife may raise not only blossoms but good rich herbs to feed her family.'* But it is proving increasingly difficult to do.

HERE'S AN IDEA FOR YOU...

If you're buying a home, pay as much deposit as possible. Avoid introductory loan rates; and if your interest rate is cut, pay the same amount so you reduce the debt faster. As little as £30 a month over the minimum would knock £10,000 off a £200,000 loan and reduce the term by fourteen months.

25 INSURE FOR THE FUTURE

According to Arkad the sixth cure for a lean purse is to,
'Provide in advance for the needs of thy growing age and the protection of thy family. It behooves a man to make preparation for a suitable income in the days to come, when he is no longer young.'

DEFINING IDEA...

For almost seventy years the life insurance industry has been a smug sacred cow feeding the public a steady line of sacred bull.
~ RALPH NADER, AMERICAN AUTHOR AND POLICAL ACTIVIST

Arkad predicts, *'In my mind rests a belief that some day wise-thinking men will devise a plan to insure against death whereby many men pay in but a trifling sum regularly, the aggregate making a handsome sum for the family of each member who passeth to the beyond. This do I see as something desirable and which I could highly recommend...'*

That day has, of course, arrived. Clason's enthusiasm for insurance comes through on several occasions. So much so, that you have to wonder whether he was on commission from the banks and insurance companies through which he distributed millions of his original pamphlets...

Insurance as we know it today started in seventeenth-century England. In 1688 merchants, ship-owners and underwriters met at Lloyd's Coffee House in London to discuss and do business. By the end of the eighteenth century, Lloyd's had become one of the first modern insurance companies and is still in operation today.

These days you can insure just about anything, but do you really need to? An estimated 4500 men winced so badly when Lorraine Bobbit took a sharp knife to her cheating husband's tackle that they have insured against meeting the same fate. For just $150 a year they can rest assured that they will be compensated with $1.5 million should their partners take a violent dislike to their behaviour. Personally, I'd have thought that if you were in a relationship with someone who had a penchant for carving knives you would be better off tempering your philandering ways or just leaving.

Or what about alien abduction? If you have concerns about being beamed up by little green men, then fear not – yes, you can insure against it happening. About 20,000 people sleep easier at night knowing that should aliens decide to conduct experiments on them, the insurance company will be on hand to dish out $1.5 million. Considering how difficult it is to convince an insurance company that you spilled milk on your laptop under an accidental damage policy, it strikes me that any returning abductees may have a little trouble proving what happened to them, however...

Silliness aside, having too much insurance is just a waste of money. However, investing in insurance to protect yourself and your family is sensible. Arkad concludes by saying *'no man can afford not to insure a treasure for his old age and the protection of his family, no matter how prosperous his business and his investments may be.'*

HERE'S AN IDEA FOR YOU...

Thoroughly check your insurance policies; focus attention on the smaller than normal print at the back. Insurance companies bank on the fact that by the time you get to the exclusions you'll have lost the will to live. Read the small print – especially the exclusions – and make an informed decision about the policy's validity.

26 INCREASE YOUR ABILITY TO EARN

On the last day of teaching Arkad told his students that the seventh and last remedy for a lean purse is to, *'cultivate thy own powers, to study and become wiser, to become more skillful, to so act as to respect thyself. The more of wisdom we know, the more we may earn.'*

Arkad tells the story of a young man who came to ask for his advice: *'...six times within two moons have I approached my master to request my pay be increased, but without success. No man can go oftener than that.'*

DEFINING IDEA...

If a man empties his purse into his head, no man can take it away from him. An investment in knowledge always pays the best interest.
~ BENJAMIN FRANKLIN

All too often we are focused on what we will get rather than what we will give. We expect to be rewarded first and prove our worth later. We expect to get a pay rise each year just for turning up and convince ourselves that if the bosses want more then they will just have to pay more. But why on earth would they? We have to be better at our work, consistently do more than is asked of us and in the fullness of time we will have the reward – and not the other way around.

When Arkad started out as a scribe he realised quickly that he had to improve to warrant more money: *'With reasonable promptness my increased skill was rewarded, nor was it necessary for me to go six times to my master to request recognition.'*

Actions always speak louder than words. This idea was never more obvious than in the UK TV show *The Apprentice* where no-nonsense, self-made millionaire Sir Alan Sugar puts sixteen aspiring (often deluded) tycoons through their business paces to see who will get a job in his organisation. In the fourth series the highlight was Michael Sophocles – a self-professed 'born salesman' who attempted to sell Ferrari rental packages in a street market. I can see it now: 'Four big baking potatoes, a punnet of strawberries and a half-day hire of that Ferrari, please…' How he survived to the last six contestants is a complete mystery, but eventually the incongruence between what he said he was and what he could demonstrate he actually was became undeniable.

Deliver your best performance, learn all you can so you can improve that performance and not only will feel better about yourself but you are sure to be noticed and rewarded. If you're not, then move on. Don't shout about your ability; demonstrate it instead.

Arkad assures his students, '*Always do the affairs of man change and improve because keen-minded men seek greater skill that they may better serve those upon whose patronage they depend. Therefore, I urge all men to be in the front rank of progress and not to stand still, lest they be left behind.*'

HERE'S AN IDEA FOR YOU…

If you want to make more money at work, improve your performance. Learn how to do your job better, faster and more efficiently. If you see a part of the system that could be improved then speak up and suggest a solution. Eventually this will be noticed. You'll never get more by giving less.

27 PAY DEBTS PROMPTLY

In closing his lesson on the seven cures to a lean purse Arkad offers three further things a man must do if he is to respect himself. One is, *'He must pay his debts with all the promptness within his power, not purchasing that for which he is unable to pay.'*

DEFINING IDEA...

Credit buying is much like being drunk; the buzz happens immediately, and it gives you a lift. The hangover comes the day after.

~ DR JOYCE BROTHERS, AMERICAN PSYCHOLOGIST AND ADVICE COLUMNIST

In the UK, the chief executives of the five leading credit card issuers appeared before the Commons Treasury committee in 2003 to answer complaints about their charges. The committee wanted banks to supply clearer information. A study by Royal & Sun Alliance showed that 62% of credit card holders had no idea of their standard annual percentage rate (APR), which can be up to five times above base rate.

Matt Barrett, the Barclays chief executive, attracted particular criticism after admitting, 'I do not borrow on credit cards. It is too expensive. I have four young children. I give them advice not to pile up debts on their credit cards.' Surprising, perhaps, but at least he was honest! He conceded that a Barclaycard customer making the minimum monthly repayment might take more than ten years to pay off the balance.

The only way to use a credit card usefully is to pay off the balance in full every month, which is what Matt Barrett and about 50% of his customers do. For the remaining 4.5 million customers – well, they sink further and further into the mire of debt.

Lenders are the only ones getting rich because of credit cards. In December 2007 the total UK credit card debt stood at £54.9 billion. The collective limit on the cards in circulation was £177 billion. In February 2008, the average interest rate on credit card lending was 17.31% – at the time that was 12.06% above the base rate!

Matt Barrett was slammed for his comments in what the media described as a 'Ratner-style gaffe'. But who's the idiot? The head of UK's largest issuer of credit cards who openly admits he doesn't rack up debt on his own product because it's too expensive or the millions of credit card customers who do? Think about it for a second. If Richard Branson refused to fly Virgin Atlantic but chose Qantas instead, wouldn't you think twice about booking a ticket with Virgin?

Take Arkad's advice and minimise your debt. Besides, money worries are officially bad for your health. Believe it or not Dr Roger Henderson, GP and mental health expert, has identified Money Sickness Syndrome (MSS), adding that 43% of the UK adult population is adversely affected by stress and anxiety caused by financial problems. Dr Henderson says, 'Money worries can cause significant problems in relationships, and people who suffer are often in worse health than those who are in control of their finances.'

HERE'S AN IDEA FOR YOU...

Find out what APR you are paying on all your credit cards. Visit one of the online comparison sites to find a cheaper APR, thoroughly check the fine print to ensure the rate is not just introductory and move your debt. Shop around – it could save you hundreds.

28 MAKE A WILL

Arkad suggests that the second essential aspect for ensuring self-respect is, *'He must make a will of record that, in case the gods call him, proper and honorable division of his property be accomplished'*. Even in ancient times looking after those left behind was considered a priority.

DEFINING IDEA...

But thousands die without or this or that, Die, and endow a college, or a cat: To some, indeed, Heav'n grants the happier fate, T'enrich a bastard, or a son they hate.

~ ALEXANDER POPE, ENGLISH POET

According to the UK's Inland Revenue, the majority of British adults don't have a valid will. Most simply haven't got around to it because they either assume that it will cost too much or they believe their affairs are not complex enough to warrant one.

What they don't realise, however, is that not having a will could potentially mean your estate goes to the government. If you die without making a will ('intestate') then you or your loved ones lose all control over the division of your assets. Instead, strict laws that govern deceased estates come into effect and your wishes could be ignored.

If you are married or in a civil partnership then your partner will not automatically be entitled to everything. Rather, they will receive the first £125,000 of the assets tax-free (unless there are no children, in which case this figure rises to £200,000), along with personal effects. But anything left over goes to children, grandchildren, parents then finally siblings (although half-siblings get nothing).

Often people assume their estate will go to their kids, especially if they re-marry. This is not the case, however, and unless you make a will detailing your explicit instructions then your assets will be distributed according to the law. So if you don't get on with your family and want to leave your estate to your gerbils – make a will… You can find basic information on government websites.

Now, it's also worth noting that if you die without a will the tax implications can be disastrous for those left behind, especially if you are not married to your partner. According to the tax department, there are numerous cases every year of individuals being forced out of the family home due to their inability to pay their tax liability.

One of the strangest wills ever written was by Charles Vance Millar who notoriously left the bulk of his estate to the Toronto woman who had the greatest number of children in the ten years after his death, resulting in the 'Great Stork Derby'. Attempts to invalidate it by his would-be heirs were unsuccessful, and the bulk of Millar's fortune eventually went to four women.

There are also countless examples of people ignoring relatives for cats, dogs and even chimpanzees. But if you want to look after your family and ensure they don't have to endure financial difficulties as well as emotional ones, then follow Arkad's advice and make a will.

HERE'S AN IDEA FOR YOU…

If you don't already have one, type 'make a will' into any search engine; you'll be presented with millions of pages. Many websites offer free forms to download and complete, or you can simply complete the forms online and have your will returned in a few days for a reasonable fee.

29 SHOW COMPASSION TO OTHERS IN NEED

Arkad states the last essential aspect of ensuring self-respect is, _'He must have compassion upon those who are injured and smitten by misfortune and aid them within reasonable limits. He must do deeds of thoughtfulness to those dear to him.'_ Extending a helping hand to others is still important.

Take the UK. Considering there are over 200,000 charities in operation across the country, Britons must surely be compassionate. Between Children in Need's Pudsey Bear and being systematically hijacked by charity muggers (a.k.a. chuggers) on high streets up and down the land, they donate millions to charity every year.

DEFINING IDEA...
If you want others to be happy, practise compassion. If you want to be happy, practise compassion.
~ THE DALAI LAMA

However, according to Lord Joffe, the British have actually been getting less charitable over the past fifteen years. Apparently, despite rising average incomes and the doubling of personal wealth, charitable donations have dropped by 25%. Most Britons give away just 7p of every £10 they earn. Interestingly enough, it's not the rich who dig deep for something like Comic Relief, it's those people who don't necessarily have the spare cash to do so. Perhaps the spate of donation scandals has fuelled latent concerns about just how much gets to its intended destination, or perhaps the rich are just mean and that's how they got rich in the first place...

Thankfully, not all rich people are mean, and there are several examples of outstanding generosity. One of the most famous philanthropists of all time was Andrew Carnegie. Having amassed a fortune in steel, he spent the second half of his life giving it away.

In recent times billionaires and long-time friends Bill Gates and Warren Buffet are carrying on that honourable tradition. In June 2008 Bill Gates stepped down from the day-to-day operation of Microsoft to focus on his work with the world's largest philanthropic organisation, the $30 billion Bill and Melinda Gates Foundation. The foundation focuses on fighting such diseases such as malaria, HIV–AIDS and tuberculosis, and on improving US libraries and high schools.

In 2006 Warren Buffet pledged to gradually give away 85% of his wealth in favour of five foundations. At the time of the announcement the gift was worth over $40 billion, making it the largest philanthropic gift in history. However, because the donation is in Berkshire Hathaway B shares and is also staggered over several years, the price of the shares on the date of each gift will determine its dollar value. Considering that the value in those shares has already increased by over $1000 per share since Buffet's announcement, the final value of the donation is likely to be far more than $40 billion. Five-sixths of the shares will go to the Gates Foundation, where Buffett will join Bill and Melinda Gates as the third trustee.

Whether we are rich or not, Arkad advises that we show compassion to others and, wherever possible, should help those less fortunate than ourselves.

HERE'S AN IDEA FOR YOU...

There are plenty of great causes that need support and many are not even charities. Perhaps there something like a volunteer organisation visiting old people in your area. Offering either some time or some money could make a real difference. And helping others makes you feel better too.

30 WHAT WERE YOU TAUGHT IN SCHOOL?

In Chapter 4 of the Richest Man in Babylon we meet Arkad again. This time he is teaching in the '... *Temple of Learning where the wisdom of the past was expounded by voluntary teachers and where subjects of popular interest were discussed in open forums.'* Arkad taught most evenings.

Clason talks about the fact that there was no formal schooling in Babylon. But there was still a centre of learning and a very practical one at that. Although it is rarely mentioned in the history books it *'ranked in importance with the palace of the King, the Hanging Gardens and the temples of the gods'.*

DEFINING IDEA...

I loved learning, it was school I hated. I used to cut school to go learn something.

– ERIC JENSEN, AUTHOR

Today we have schools and colleges but are we really any better off? Did you know, for example, that the idea for compulsory schooling came from the Indian caste system? In India people are born into a particular station in life. The top 5% are known as 'twice born' and they are educated and wealthy. The remaining 95% are born into menial labour and include the group known as the 'untouchables'. After visiting India a young Anglican chaplain called Andrew Bell noticed that Hinduism had created a mass schooling institution for children that taught 'willing servility' and recognised the possibilities of such a system in creating a docile workforce for the industrial revolution.

School as we know it was the result. The powers that be decided that schooled ignorance was better than unschooled stupidity. So schools were created to 'teach' people how to fit into a system that desperately needed them. In America, very wealthy men such as Rockefeller exerted huge influence on schools at the time. In the first mission statement of Rockefeller's General Education Board the true intention of school was revealed...

'In our dreams... people yield themselves with perfect docility to our molding hands... We shall not try to make these people or any of their children into philosophers or men of learning or men of science. We have not to raise up from among them authors, educators, poets or men of letters. We shall not search for embryo great artists, painters, musicians, nor lawyers, doctors, preachers, politicians, statesmen, of whom we have ample supply. The task we set before ourselves is very simple... we will organize children... and teach them to do in a perfect way the things their fathers and mothers are doing in an imperfect way.'

Makes you think, doesn't it? Don't assume school will prepare you for life. It doesn't – it prepares you to follow rules, get good grades and slot into a pre-packaged position so you can work to make someone else rich.

The fact is, learning happens best when it is voluntary and relevant to life. Arkad reminds us of just how advanced Babylon was. Within the walls of the Temple of Learning in Babylon *all men met as equals. The humblest of slaves could dispute with impunity the opinions of a prince of the royal house'*.

HERE'S AN IDEA FOR YOU...
Write down five strengths you have, and how you could improve them and perhaps make money from them. People rarely get rich working for someone else – time to start thinking outside the box.

31 IS THERE A WAY TO ATTRACT GOOD LUCK?

Arkad is asked by one of his students at the Temple *'Is there a way to attract good luck?'* The man tells his story: *'This day I have been lucky, for I have found a purse in which there are pieces of gold. To continue to be lucky is my great desire.'*

Of course he forgets that the man who lost the purse could just as easily have told the other side of the tale, seeking answers about how to avoid such bad fortune…

DEFINING IDEA…

Whenever you see a gaming table be sure to know fortune is not there. Rather she is always in the company of industry.

~ OLIVER GOLDSMITH, WRITER

Arkad, however, feels the topic is worthy of discussion and the conversation inevitably turns to gambling. *'When a man speaketh of luck is it not natural that his thoughts turn to the gaming tables? Is it not there we find many men courting the favor of the goddess in hope she will bless them with rich winnings?'*

Because the gambling industry is so fragmented, it's very difficult to get any hard and fast figures about how much is being spent. The UK's Betting Office Licensees Association estimates that global gambling in all forms is worth around US$1,000 billion. According to the British Gambling Prevalence Survey 2007 conducted by the National Centre of Social Research, the amount retained by operators after payment of winnings – but before the deduction of costs – had increased from just over £7 billion in 1999–2000 to just under £10 billion in 2007.

That's a lot of money and validates Arkad's point that *'The game is so arranged that it will always favor the keeper… Few players realize how certain are the game keeper's profits and how uncertain are their own chances to win.'*

According to the report up to 378,000 people in Britain have a gambling problem and it's more prevalent among men than women. Being divorced doesn't help either, although the study didn't speculate about whether divorce leads to problem gambling, or whether problem gambling leads to divorce. But I'd hazard a guess it's the latter.

The number of ways in which we can lose our money these days is mind-numbing: casinos, horse races, greyhounds, lottery, football pools, scratch cards, bingo and slot machines – in Australia you can even play 'two-up' and bet on the toss of a coin! But whilst gambling methods may have become more sophisticated than the gaming tables of Babylon, the result is still the same.

Arkad reminds us that Lady Luck *'is a goddess of love and dignity whose pleasure it is to aid those who are in need and to reward those who are deserving. I look to find her, not at the gaming tables or the races where men lose more gold than they win but in other places where the doings of men are more worthwhile and more worthy of reward.'*

HERE'S AN IDEA FOR YOU...
If you go to the races for the day, don't take your credit card or your cash card. Take cash – once that's spent, that's all you can lose. If you're lucky you'll save a little for a taxi home; if not, you can enjoy a nice long walk while you contemplate your loss.

32 GOOD LUCK REWARDS THOSE WHO ACCEPT OPPORTUNITY

In the discussion about luck Arkad suggests, *'Now, suppose we consider our trades and businesses. Is it not natural if we conclude a profitable transaction to consider it not good luck but a just reward for our efforts? I am inclined to think we may be overlooking the gifts of the goddess.'*

Perhaps luck is not down to random chance, but to recognising and making the most of any opportunities that arise. Certainly history is littered with examples, including those of opportunities missed…

DEFINING IDEA…
Luck is a matter of preparation meeting opportunity.
~ OPRAH WINFREY

In 1885, the French inventor Augustine Le Prince developed a prototype for a motion picture camera. In 1888 he received the first patent both in France and the United States and in 1890 he demonstrated it to officials at the Paris Opera House. Despite it being well received, he returned to his workshop to perfect the device. He later disappeared in suspicious circumstances and Thomas Edison is now more widely acknowledged as the inventor of the motion picture camera. If Le Prince had seized the opportunity to make his discovery known after Paris, rather than seeking perfection, he and not Edison would have gone down in history for the invention.

In recent years Yahoo's missed opportunity to buy Google is now famous. Google's founders Larry Page and Sergey Brin called on their friend and Yahoo! founder David Filo to sell their fledgling business. Although Filo agreed that the technology was solid, he decided not to get involved adding,

'When it's fully developed and scalable, let's talk again'. Google, however, found the necessary funding and by the time it was 'fully developed and scalable' the opportunity had passed. In the space of a decade Google has gone from a garage start-up to one of the most successful businesses of all time, and shows no signs of slowing.

In my own life seizing an opportunity launched a career in writing. A friend of mine I was doing some work with told me of someone he knew in the US who was looking for a writer to help him rework his manuscript. At the time I was a discontented marketing consultant harbouring aspirations as a writer. The man in question was Blair Singer – an internationally renowned speaker specialising in sales. I spoke to Blair and said that I'd rework a few chapters and that if he liked the result we'd do the book and if he didn't then it wouldn't him cost anything. He loved it and *SalesDogs* was the result. Today that book is an international bestseller in Robert Kiyosaki's *Rich Dad Advisor* series.

Good luck is therefore perhaps more accurately described as a cause and effect result that occurs when opportunities are recognised and acted upon. As Arkad points out, *'Perhaps she [Goddess Luck] really does assist us when we do not appreciate her generosity.'*

HERE'S AN IDEA FOR YOU...

List all the events or circumstances that you consider to be lucky and unlucky in the last two months. Looking back, can you trace them to something you did or initiated? Is it possible that good luck was not luck at all but good planning and the recognition of opportunity? Is the reverse also true?

33 DON'T DELAY – PROCRASTINATION DESTROYS OPPORTUNITY

On the subject of lost opportunities through procrastination one of Arkad's students laments, *'We mortals are changeable. Alas, I must say more apt to change our minds when right than wrong. Wrong, we are stubborn indeed. Right, we are prone to vacillate and let opportunity escape.'*

DEFINING IDEA...
Procrastination is opportunity's natural assassin.
– VICTOR KIAM, BUSINESSMAN AND ENTREPRENEUR

When Google's founders, Sergey Brin and Larry Page, were unable to interest the major portal players of the day they decided to go it alone. But they did need money. So they wrote up a business plan and went looking for an angel investor. As chance would have it, their first visit was to Andy Bechtolsheim, one of the founders of Sun Microsystems. However, he was pressed for time. After a dawn demonstration delivered on a porch in Palo Alto, Bechtolsheim recognised the phenomenal opportunity that Google offered. But because he was in a hurry, he simply suggested, 'Instead of us discussing all the details, why don't I just write you a cheque?' He then handed over a cheque for $100,000 made out to Google Inc. Bechtolsheim obviously didn't suffer from procrastination. His foresight and shrewd appreciation for opportunity, especially in the technology area, has made him one of the most successful angel investors ever.

As for Sergey Brin and Larry Page, they were caught by surprise by this swift response. Whilst they happily accepted the cheque, it remained in a desk drawer for two weeks while they incorporated the company and opened a bank account into which they could deposit it. The rest, as they say, is history.

Every business success book is chock full of stories expounding the virtues of seizing opportunity versus procrastination. But working out which event is a real opportunity and which should definitely be procrastinated upon isn't always as easy as it looks. And rather less easy to find are examples where procrastination actually saved a fortune or the grasping of an apparent opportunity led to disaster.

It's a quandary I still grapple with. For example, I was presented with an opportunity to buy tickets to the Sydney 2008 Bledisloe Cup (a rugby union game between Australia and New Zealand). I was heading there for a visit so decided to take the chance and purchase the tickets even though they were expensive. My lack of procrastination actually resulted in me paying significantly more money for the tickets than I need have done. Needless to say, I was annoyed for days! Granted, it's not a life and death decision – but working out when an opportunity really is an opportunity isn't always as easy as the self-help books would have us believe.

Nonetheless Arkad warns, *'In listening to [procrastination] we do become our own worst enemies'.* The fable reminds us, *'Opportunity waits for no man. Today it is here; soon it is gone. Therefore, delay not!'*

HERE'S AN IDEA FOR YOU...

Procrastination can be an instinctive reluctance to get involved, or it can be fear. How do you tell a chance and a potential disaster apart? Well, don't get involved in things you don't understand. Do your research, verify the details, assess the risk and trust your instincts. It works for Warren Buffett...

34 PROVE YOUR WORTH

In The Richest Man in Babylon's fifth chapter, 'The Five Laws of Gold', Arkad appears again. 'In Babylon it is the custom, as you know, that the sons of wealthy fathers live with their parents in expectation of inheriting the estate.' Arkad did not approve of this custom. Instead he sent his son, Nomasir, away to prove himself.

'My son, it is my desire that thou succeed to my estate. Thou must, however, first prove that thou art capable of wisely handling it. Therefore, I wish that thou go out into the world and show thy ability both to acquire gold and to make thyself respected among men.'

Maybe doubts arose following the Internet sex tape, or perhaps it was the endless partying, or the twenty-two days in jail with promises of new leaves being turned over which never materialised that prompted Barron Hilton to rethink the division of his estate. Certainly there appears to be little evidence regarding either respect or the wise handling of gold where his granddaughter Paris is concerned. Although speculation that Barron Hilton was unimpressed with her behaviour was never confirmed, in December 2007 he announced he would be placing a majority of his £1.15 billion fortune in the Conrad N. Hilton Foundation. This was a decision that slashed Paris Hilton's potential inheritance from an expected £50 million to a 'however will she manage' £2.5 million.

In January 2008, Nigella Lawson was roasted in the UK's media when comments she made were taken out of context. As a result she was accused of wishing to disinherit her children from her estimated £15 million fortune. When asked by *My Weekly* magazine what she hoped her children would learn from her, Lawson actually said, 'To know that I am working and that you have to work in order to earn money. I am determined that my children should have no financial security. It ruins people not having to earn money.' And from anecdotes and historical fact she's absolutely right. Her belief that everyone – no matter how rich their parents – should learn the virtues of working to earn a living is valid and something consistently repeated in Clason's little book.

Luckily for Nomasir, his father gave him good advice and a bag of gold – and after some bitter lessons he returned triumphant ten years later. Clason notes in this fable that if you ask most people if they prefer gold or wisdom they want the gold. *'It is the same with the sons of wealthy men. Give them a choice of gold and wisdom – what do they do? Ignore the wisdom and waste the gold. On the morrow they wail because they have no more gold.' Yet, 'Gold is reserved for those who know its laws and abide by them.'*

HERE'S AN IDEA FOR YOU...

If you have made money through your hard work and creativity then you should enjoy it. Instead of spoiling your children with handouts, encourage them to get a Saturday job or a paper round. At the very least, swap their pocket money for chores. The sooner they learn that money doesn't grow on trees, the better for both parties.

35 INVEST WITH WISE MEN

Although the five laws of gold outlined in the chapter of the same name are all repeated elsewhere, it still reiterates sound advice. After losing money to scoundrels Nomasir, *'recognized an opportunity to abide by the third law and invest my savings under the guidance of wise men'*.

Idea 22 reminded us of how gullible some people can be, but what about when you invest with men that should have been wise?

DEFINING IDEA...

Wisdom is like electricity. There is no permanently wise man, but men capable of wisdom, who, being put into certain company, or other favorable conditions, become wise for a short time, as glasses rubbed acquire electric power for a while.

~ RALPH WALDO EMERSON

No doubt those investing in Société Générale, France's second largest bank, were comforted by its long history and solid track record. They would have assumed that wise men were indeed looking after their investment. So it must have come as a surprise when it was reported in January 2008 that Jérôme Kerviel, a Société Générale trader, had single-handedly lost £3.7 billion.

Thirty-one year old Kerviel was a junior trader making a relatively modest salary of £70,000 a year. He joined Société Générale in 2000 as a clerk, processing and recording the trades on the trading floor. He worked his way up to a job on the futures desk where he hedged the bank's position on European equity markets. This essentially meant that he was supposed to balance the bank's risk so that if something went down and the bank lost money he had other positions that went up to cover the shortfall. But Kerviel was only betting one way.

Over a year he had bet more than the entire bank's market capitalisation on movements in the European stock market. He had obtained a thorough understanding of the bank's security control systems and, more importantly, how to bypass them. Initially he was quite successful but it didn't last.

The market crashed following the announcement of a $150 billion tax-cutting package to boost the US economy. Already nervous about an impending recession caused by the financial fall-out of the US sub-prime problem, markets fell around the world and the FTSE 100 index fell 5.5% in the biggest one-day drop since September 11 2001. Kerviel's positions worsened as the market deteriorated, turning a potential £1.1 billion loss into an even more colossal £3.7 billion one.

Parallels were naturally drawn in the media between Kerviel and Nick Leeson – the 'rogue trader' responsible for the collapse of Barings Bank in 1995. He was vilified for his £860 million loss and spent six and a half years in a Singapore prison. Neither he nor Kerviel profited personally from their trades. Despite assurances that this sort of thing could never happen again, it did – and many 'wise men' ended up looking anything but.

It would seem that investing with wise men can sometimes be harder than it sounds. As Nomasir reminds us, *'Without wisdom, gold is quickly lost.'*

HERE'S AN IDEA FOR YOU...

If you are investing in the stock market, remember that even blue-chip companies can come unstuck. It's better to diversify your investments so that you spread your risk. Also take the long view – a paper loss is only a real loss if you sell the shares.

36 CHOOSE ACTION OVER REGRET

'Our unwise acts follow us to plague and torment us. Alas, they cannot be forgotten. In the front rank of the torments that do follow us are the memories of the things we should have done, of the opportunities which came to us and we took not.'

Although, *'Our wise acts accompany us through life to please us and to help us'*, it's the cock-ups that seem to haunt us the most.

DEFINING IDEA...
Only put off until tomorrow what you are willing to die having left undone.
~ PABLO PICASSO

Talk about Black Monday and the blood will drain from even the most experienced stock market trader's face. On Monday 19 October 1987 stock markets all around the world crashed. It began in Hong Kong, travelled west through international time zones to Europe and then on to the US where $500 billion evaporated from the Dow Jones Industrial Average index. In the UK, the FTSE lost £63 billion in value. The rest of the world fared no better, and often worse. There were many theories about why the crash happened but everyone agreed that market psychology had played a huge part. People simply panicked.

All, that is, except the smart money. Savvy traders recognised the constant opportunity inherent in the stock market to capitalise on fear and greed and the irrational behaviour of the masses. They knew that nothing negative had actually happened to the companies – most of them were as strong as ever and would bounce back – so they snapped up undervalued stock at rock-bottom prices. Almost exactly the same thing happened following the September 11 stock market crash.

A more intimate portrayal of regret and missed opportunity can be witnessed several nights a week in Britain on the TV show *Deal or No Deal*. Contestants on the programme choose one of twenty-two identical sealed boxes containing prize money ranging in value from a single penny to £250,000. The contestant chooses boxes to remove from the game and after each round must decide whether to play on or accept the banker's offer. What's really interesting is that someone who accepts an offer of £20,000 but then finds there was a huge sum of money in their box invariably looks more distraught than the person who ends up with the penny. Perhaps it's the knowledge that they had an opportunity in their grasp and they failed to capitalise on it.

This goes to verify Clason's point. It's not the things we do that we regret the most, it is the things we don't do. It's the regret for missed opportunities that wakes us up in a cold sweat ten years later. Those are the moments that can turn us bitter with disappointment, moments of weakness where fear got the better of us and we chickened out. There are, of course, times where we do take the plunge and it doesn't work out but the very act of trying seems to ease the failure. It's inaction that bruises the soul.

HERE'S AN IDEA FOR YOU...

Write down your biggest regret on a piece of paper. Then write anything positive to come from the experience on one side, negative things on the other. By crystallising the experience, you'll not only be able to call upon the torment to propel you forward, but also realise that there were positive aspects to it.

37 INTERNET RICHES

Mathon is the gold lender of Babylon. On receiving a visitor he smiles a friendly greeting. *'What indiscretions hast thou done that thou shouldst seek the lender of gold? Hast thou been unlucky at the gaming table? Or hath some plump dame entangled thee?'*

DEFINING IDEA...

The Internet is becoming the town square of the global village of tomorrow.

~ BILL GATES

It appears that men have been getting themselves into trouble in the same ways for thousands of years. Perhaps it's not a coincidence, then, when we look at modern times and find that by far the most lucrative sectors of the Internet are gambling and porn...

The meteoric rise of online poker in recent years has ensured that the only consistent 'full house' is at Gamblers Anonymous. Millions of people are glued to their flat-screen monitors in the wee hours of the morning, playing Texas Hold'em with their newfound friends from as far afield as Vladivostok, New York or Hong Kong.

Although not considered quite so sexy as games like poker, bingo is now also firmly entrenched in the online gambling scene. Started in 1530, when Italy launched a lottery that formed the basis of the game we know today, bingo really came of age in the UK following the 1968 Gaming Act. Increased broadband coverage and the national smoking ban, prohibiting players from puffing away as they filled in their cards, resulted in more and more people deserting the bingo halls for the online experience.

The sight of a hardened gambler sitting alone in a casino has always smacked of desperation but that stigma no longer applies when the Internet has provided easy, relatively anonymous access to gambling in the privacy of your own home. This isn't good news for many and is shifting the demographic of gambling, with an increasing number of women getting involved.

The consequences can be extreme. In 2007 a UK school headmaster killed himself after losing his £250,000 home and running up £100,000 debts from Internet gambling. A woman in Exeter was sent to prison after stealing £26,000 in four weeks from her employer to feed her addiction to online poker and Internet betting.

(As for the 'plump dames', I'm told there are sites dedicated to them too!)

Disregarding the tacky, sleazy and just plain stupid for a second, the Internet is nothing short of a revolution. The opportunities it offers for making money and linking to global markets is phenomenal. It's hard to believe that the first web page was created as recently as 1990, although its development has grown exponentially in the last decade. Today it is both brilliant and despicable; like the rest of life, it operates as a dichotomy and allows the very best of what is human to flourish as well as the very worst. It offers simultaneous access to unparalleled opportunity and unparalleled destruction – and which one you choose is up to you.

HERE'S AN IDEA FOR YOU...

If you are in business then you must have a website. Check out open-source software such as DotNetNuke and Joomla, which offer free or low-cost templates for building a professional site. It's easy – and the tools give you complete access and control, so you don't have to pay a webmaster to fix a typo.

38 NEVER LEND MONEY TO FRIENDS AND FAMILY!

In Chapter 6 of *The Richest Man in Babylon*, 'The Gold Lender of Babylon', Clason recalls Rodan's story. He has been given fifty pieces of gold by the King and laments, *'I am beseeched each hour the sun doth travel across the sky by those who wish to share it with me'*.

Rodan, a spear maker, is soon inundated by requests for his money. In desperation he seeks the wise advice of Mathon, the gold lender of Babylon. Mathon tells Rodan, on hearing of his troubles, *'That is natural. More men want gold than have it and would wish one who comes by it easily to divide.'*

Many a lottery jackpot winner has experienced this phenomenon as family, friends (long lost and otherwise), strangers and good causes line up for a slice. It seems that the first thing most big winners need is an unlisted phone number. As for Rodan, his angst is because his much-loved sister wants him to set her husband up as a trader. Only the man has no experience as a trader.

Lending money to family and friends is fraught with dangers. There is rarely a happy outcome unless proper investigation takes place beforehand and the investment stands up to thorough scrutiny. Without that scrutiny, unmet expectations can lead to trouble – if the deal goes well, then there may be arguments about the allocation of profits; if it goes badly, then there are sure to be recriminations. The only way to successfully navigate these traditionally choppy waters is through extreme due diligence and open and honest communication.

You should never invest in anything without thoroughly checking the facts and figures. You need to assure yourself that the people involved have the experience and ability to do what they say they will do and that applies doubly for friends and family. Don't let loyalty or emotional attachment cloud your judgment or common sense.

You have to have an open and honest discussion that involves details of what will happen in the worst-case scenario as well as the best. How will you get your money out if your circumstances change? What will happen if they lose everything? You must have a legal contract, which covers repayment and dividend expectations, and an exit strategy. These sorts of investments offer a great deal more risk because emotion is involved and you run the risk of permanently damaging the relationships in the process.

Mathon reminds Rodan, *'Gold bringeth unto its possessor responsibility and a changed position with his fellow men. It bringeth fear lest he lose it or it be tricked away from him. It bringeth a feeling of power and ability to do good. Likewise, it bringeth opportunities whereby his very good intentions may bring him into difficulties.'*

HERE'S AN IDEA FOR YOU...
Don't invest with family and friends unless you have thoroughly vetted the opportunity and discussed all the possible outcomes – including losing your money. The investment needs to be viable and sensible; if it's not, then don't get involved, regardless of who is asking.

39 GOOD DEBT VS. BAD DEBT

Mathon offers Rodan advice on who is most likely to repay their debts: *'If they borrow for purposes that bring money back to them, I find it so. But if they borrow because of their indiscretions, I warn thee to be cautious if thou wouldst ever have thy gold back in hand again.'*

DEFINING IDEA...

Today, there are three kinds of people: the haves, the have-nots, and the have-not-paid-for-what-they-haves.

~ EARL WILSON, POLITICIAN

In modern times, this idea is expressed as good debt and bad debt. Basically good debt is anything that is making you money, so something like an investment property would be classed as good debt. The idea is simple – buy a property, rent it out and have that rental repay your mortgage and provide a residual income. You end up with a valuable asset and someone else has paid off your mortgage.

It is this idea that spawned the buy-to-let boom. For many years, few people had property aspirations beyond owning their own home. But for some astute investors, property represented a huge opportunity. Then the rest of the population cottoned on and the term 'buy to let' was coined.

But things can go wrong, especially if you pay too much for the property in the first place. In June 2008 Bradford and Bingley, one of Britain's biggest buy-to-let lenders, announced it had made an £8 million pre-tax loss between January and April, compared with a £108 million profit in the same three months in 2007. The global credit crunch, rising inflation and depressed consumer confidence had, at least for a time, taken the shine off the buy to let market. Nonetheless, investing in property is a long-term strategy and is still classed as good debt.

Bad debt, on the other hand, is anything that doesn't make you money. That means credit cards, store cards and unsecured loans are all bad debt.

Credit is a vital part of business. As Mathon says, *'Good merchants are an asset to our city and it profits me to aid them to keep trade moving that Babylon be prosperous.'*

One of the problems traditionally experienced by businesses is access to funds for start-up or expansion. A new business will not have the necessary track record or assets to offer banks as collateral, and even if a business has been established for a while the rules for lending can be difficult to negotiate. This inability to access cash can lead to businesses 'bootstrapping' – using personal credit cards as a source of funding. Though tempting, this is never wise and still constitutes bad debt.

Mathon warns that bad debt will plunge you into *'a deep pit into which one may descend quickly and where one may struggle vainly…It is a pit of sorrow and regrets where the brightness of the sun is overcast and night is made unhappy by restless sleeping.'*

HERE'S AN IDEA FOR YOU…

Ever hear 'Can I borrow some money?' from your kids? Well, make sure they pay you back. If you feel like a tightwad, put repayments in their bank account – but ensure they do repay and, if necessary, add interest. The sooner kids understand that 'borrow' means 'borrow' the better. No more until the debt is cleared, either…

40 SPREAD YOUR RISK

On advising Rodan about whether to invest with his sister Mathon says *'If thee wouldst lend it so that it may earn thee more gold, then lend with caution and in many places. I like not idle gold, even less I like too much of risk.'*

DEFINING IDEA...

Diversify your investments.
~ JOHN TEMPLETON, STOCK INVESTOR

When it comes to investing there are two main camps – property and shares. The stock market enthusiasts usually like the accessibility, liquidity and speed that is available in the stock market. They like the fact that they can sell whenever they want and there are always buyers and sellers in the market. They can trade twenty-four hours a day and they don't have to deal with irritated tenants, as they might need to if they were involved with property. If they know what they are doing, they can use complex financial instruments such as options to protect their investments.

Property enthusiasts, on the other hand, don't mind leaky roofs and broken boilers and feel comforted by 'bricks and mortar'. They like the fact that property is tangible, and that for a small deposit they can control a valuable asset and use that asset to leverage their position and buy more property. They like doing property up and seeing their asset appreciate in value while someone else, in principle, pays the mortgage.

Many of the modern investment vehicles, such as managed funds and unit trusts, utilise diversification in order to spread risk. There are even property funds which allow you to benefit from owning property, including commercial property, without the hands-on involvement.

The two markets – property and shares – are linked and one will often prosper at the expense of the other in boom/bust cycles. Both offer excellent potential for return and risk management, especially when viewed over the long term.

Like so many of these things, the problem with diversification and the assessment of risk lies in the execution. How do you confidently assess risk, especially when the accepted methods of doing so have proven to be fundamentally flawed? The unravelling of the AAA risk assessment rating caused part of the financial furore of 2007–8. In the past, risk assessment fell on companies such as Standard & Poor, Moody's and Fitch and a risk rating of AAA meant the investment was solid. Triple A ratings made the sale of that investment very easy because people assumed that they were buying a low-risk, moderate-return investment. Unfortunately, they were not. The AAA element had been mixed with junk investments, therefore diluting its worth despite it still carrying the AAA rating. This was a bit like buying a solid gold ring and watching as your finger turned green.

Mathon advises against concentration of risk adding, *'I will no longer lend any of it where I am not confident that it is safe and will be returned to me.'*

HERE'S AN IDEA FOR YOU...

Invest in something you know. If you're going to invest in property, then invest locally where you know the market. If you're going to invest in the stock market, then invest in businesses and sectors where you have experience. You are far more likely to be aware of potential difficulties and make better investments.

41 BEWARE ANYTHING FLAMING!

'Be not swayed by the fantastic plans of impractical men who think they see ways to force thy gold to make earnings unusually large. Such plans are the creations of dreamers unskilled in the safe and dependable laws of trade.' **Once more Clason warns against avarice.**

Early in 2008 Credit Suisse caused a stir in an already fragile market when they announced they would have to write off £1.5 billion more than expected due to 'pricing errors'. When news emerged that it was actually 'intentional misconduct' by a handful of rogue traders, Credit Suisse must have experienced an uncomfortable feeling of déjà vu.

DEFINING IDEA...

Ambition makes the same mistake concerning power that avarice makes concerning wealth. She begins by accumulating power as a means to happiness, and she finishes by continuing to accumulate it as an end.
CHARLES CALEB COLTON, CLERIC AND WRITER

When it comes to the *fantastic plans of impractical men'*, Credit Suisse have had their fair share. In 1999 it sacked three traders for manipulating the market in the quest for 'unusually large' earnings. Perhaps a clue to the impending doom could have been picked up by the fact the trio called themselves the Flaming Ferraris after their favourite after-hours cocktail.

These and countless other scandals are so often conveniently blamed on rogue traders. But are they really that surprising? No one was complaining when Nick Leeson, the original rogue trader, was making Barings Bank millions. He could do no wrong and no one questioned if his reported profits were even possible. Or what about Jérôme Kerviel from Société Génerale? How can one person lose £3.7 billion without questions being asked?

In March 2008, the Financial Services Authority issued a rare statement to reassure the market. They suspected that a small minority of traders were deliberately spreading rumours to stir up panic selling and force share prices down so they would profit. This unscrupulous behaviour caused Halifax Bank of Scotland (HBOS) stock to dive by 17%.

According to Roger Steare, a professor of organisational ethics at Cass Business School in London, it is because of 'a systemic moral corruption within the financial services sector'. With six- and seven-figure bonuses up for grabs it is inevitable that someone somewhere is going to go too far. The system almost guarantees it. There is no personal accountability. Those involved are essentially risking other people's money, with no personal consequences when they get it wrong and breath-taking rewards if they get it right. Perhaps management doesn't want to ask too many questions when profits are being made – especially excessive, almost impossible, profits.

Even Mervyn King, the Governor of the Bank of England, attacked excessive incentives. He added that he hoped financial institutions had learned their lesson and would accept that it was now time for change following the financial meltdown of 2007–8. So forget fantastic plans and instead, *'Be conservative in what thou expect it to earn that thou mayest keep and enjoy thy treasure'.*

HERE'S AN IDEA FOR YOU...

If you must speculate in high-risk options, have a strategy. Split your investment nest egg and protect the majority. Only invest in high-risk investments with money you can comfortably lose. Take profits (if there are any) regularly, add half to your safer portfolio and start again. Don't get greedy.

42 HIGH REWARD MEANS HIGH RISK

'To hire it out with a promise of usurious returns is to invite loss. Seek to associate thyself with men and enterprises whose success is established that thy treasure may earn liberally under their skillful use and be guarded safely by their wisdom and experience.'

As we've seen in previous ideas, when it comes to high risk and high reward there is nowhere like the stock market. For professional investors who genuinely know what they are doing, then the stock market offers a great rate of return with minimal risk – but for everyone else it can be dangerous.

DEFINING IDEA...

I don't look to jump over seven-foot bars; I look around for one-foot bars that I can step over.
~ WARREN BUFFETT

The advent of stock market investing seminars has ensured an eager brigade of would-be millionaires who are entering the market mesmerised by promises of untold riches. I remember attending one of these seminars many years ago and being particularly taken with the idea of options. I found it incredible that there was a place in the world where you could sell something you didn't own and make loads of money doing it. What was not explained in the seminar was the speed at which you could also lose money using options…

Basically an option is the right, but not obligation, to buy or sell shares at a particular price in the future. Say, for example, the shares in XYZ Co are £24 but I believe the market is going up. I could buy a call option on XYZ shares that expires in one month's time at a strike price of £25 and pay a premium to the writer or seller of that contract for the privilege. In a month I check the market and if the share price has gone up to, say, £26 then I exercise my option to buy those shares and pocket the £1 difference. What's crazy is that the person who sold me that option didn't actually need to own those shares! So when I exercise the option and make my £1 a share the writer of that contract has lost £25 per share because he or she has to buy them on the open market in order to complete on the agreement. This may not sound too painful but when you consider that each contract is for a minimum of 1000 shares you can start to see just how financially lethal they can be.

On top of the profit potential, options also allow you to control shares for a fraction of the cost of actually buying them. Needless to say their *promise of usurious returns* does indeed invite loss – at a remarkable speed! As many a budding investor has found out to their cost, options can go horribly wrong and do so horribly fast. If you want to use them do as Arkad advises and *'Seek to associate thyself with men whose success is established'*.

HERE'S AN IDEA FOR YOU...

You can buy the right to control shares far more cheaply than the actual shares, so you can use options to protect the shares you do own against a drop in value, essentially betting against your own position. If the shares drop, you pick up a bonus through the option to compensate for the loss.

43 WHAT COLOUR DO YOU SEE THE WORLD?

In Chapter 8 of *The Richest Man in Babylon* we meet Dabasir the camel trader. He is talking to Tarkad who owes him and others money, and hasn't eaten for days. Dabasir asks, *'Thinkest all the world could look to a man a different color from what it is?'*

Like Tarkad, Dabasir had once been full of excuses about why he could not pay off his debts. He too had seen *'the world through a colored stone and did not realize to what degradation [he] had fallen.'* Before he was a successful camel trader he had run away from his debts, leaving Babylon in search of easy solutions, and had eventually been sold into slavery.

There is no recipe whatsoever for success or happiness. There are examples of success and failure from every walk of life. There are those people who have been born into luxury and privilege, and who have made nothing of the opportunity. Then there are those like Oprah Winfrey who, although born into poverty, conquered a white male-dominated industry and is today one of the most influential women of all time. She's also a billionaire. There are those like W Mitchell who have suffered horrendous accidents or experiences and yet have gone on – he had a motorbike accident that left him burned over 65% of his body. Then, after recovering from that terrible experience, he was involved in an plane crash that paralysed him. Mitchell tells us that 'It's not what happens to you, it's what you do about it that matters'. And he should certainly know.

In his classic old book *The Science of Getting Rich*, Wallace D. Wattles reminds us about the power of our attitudes and beliefs: 'Since belief is all-important, it behoves you to guard your thoughts, and as your beliefs will be shaped to a very great extent by the things you observe and think about, it is important that you should carefully govern to what you give your attention. If you want to become rich, you must not make a study of poverty. Things are not brought into being by thinking about their opposites.'

Any limiting beliefs you have about what is possible will just become your jailers and taint the way you view the world – if you let them. Changing your life for the better is more about attitude and determination than it is about talent, ability or luck. It starts by you believing that change is really possible.

Dabasir tells Tarkad his own story and how he turned his life around, then 'Moisture came to the eyes of the youth. He rose eagerly. *"Thou has shown me a vision; already I feel the soul of a free man surge within me".'*

HERE'S AN IDEA FOR YOU...
Write 'rich people are…' on a piece of paper; add the first thing that springs to mind. Read the sentence aloud and keep adding whatever words or phrases occur to you. Repeat on another piece for 'poor people are…'. This should illuminate some of your beliefs about money. Do they assist you in creating wealth?

44 DON'T RUN FROM DEBT

Dabasir is reprimanded by his mistress, *'If thou contentedly let the years slip by and make no effort to repay, then thou hast but the contemptible soul of a slave. No man is otherwise who cannot respect himself and no man can respect himself who does not repay honest debts.'*

DEFINING IDEA...

What can be added to the happiness of a man who is in health, out of debt, and has a clear conscience?

~ ADAM SMITH,
PHILOSOPHER AND ECONOMIST

Telling Tarkad his story Dabasir said, '*Being young and without experience I did not know that he who spends more than he earns is sowing the winds of needless self-indulgence from which he is sure to reap the whirlwinds of trouble and humiliation. So I indulged my whims for fine raiment and bought luxuries for my good wife and our home, beyond our means.*'

According to the UK government's own statistics there were 25,264 individuals in England and Wales who lived beyond their means resulting in them declaring themselves bankrupt in the first quarter of 2008. For some, bankruptcy is the only solution; for all too many it's the easy solution following years of debt with 'no effort to repay'.

The vast majority of these bankruptcies were the result of personal loans and out-of-control credit card balances and were the consequence of people systematically living beyond their means. But bankruptcy should be viewed as a last resort, not a 'get out of jail free' card. And the situation is expected to get worse with the introduction of Debt Relief Orders, which will allow low-income borrowers to declare themselves bankrupt online without attending bankruptcy court or dealing with the usual hassles and costs associated with bankruptcy.

Don't be fooled. Bankruptcy will negatively affect your ability to gain funds in the future and there are also a number of career choices from which you will be excluded. Incredibly, though, you will still be able to mange other people's money in the financial services industry or become an MP! A better solution in the UK, certainly in terms of stigma and self-respect, is an Individual Voluntary Agreement (IVA). They are more flexible and allow the debtor to write off part of the debt and negotiate with the creditor to repay the rest over an agreed period of time.

Not all bankruptcies should, however, be tarred with the same brush. Many famous entrepreneurs including H. J. Heinz, Walt Disney and Milton Hershey of the chocolate empire have experienced bankruptcy before they made their fortune. Certainly there is something nobler about getting into financial trouble by taking a calculated risk and giving 100% to a business venture than buying yet another pair of shoes and dining out seven nights a week in 'needless self-indulgence'.

Dabasir realized that running from his debts didn't erase them and chipped away at his integrity and self respect. He returned to Babylon, repaid all he owed and became a wealthy camel trader.

HERE'S AN IDEA FOR YOU…

If you're in financial difficulties seek independent advice from someone without any vested interest in potential solutions. Companies offering loan consolidation may appear to offer a convenient solution but it may not be in your best interests. Often all loan consolidation does is increase the time you'll be in debt.

45 DETERMINATION CAN SOLVE ANYTHING

'Die in the desert! Not I! We found the trail to Babylon because the soul of a free man looks at life as a series of problems to be solved and solves them, while the soul of a slave whines, "What can I do who am but a slave?"'

DEFINING IDEA...

It's not whether you get knocked down. It's whether you get up again.

~ VINCE LOMBARDI, US FOOTBALL COACH

Dabasir was deliberately given the opportunity to escape by the mistress he had befriended – and he took it. While in the desert, he collapsed after days without food and water. But something within him stirred and he tapped into his own determination. He took responsibility for his actions and made a promise to himself not only to survive but also to pay back his debts and prosper.

Wallace D. Wattles talks of the importance of willpower and determination in his little book, *The Science of Getting Rich*. 'When you know what to think and do, then you must use your will to compel yourself to think and do the right things... to use it in holding yourself to the right course. Use your mind to form a mental image of what you want and to hold that vision with faith and purpose.'

I'm sure that, following their bankruptcy, it would have been tempting for H. J. Heinz, Walt Disney and Milton Hershey to give up. But they didn't – because they were determined and committed to their goal. And the world has, by and large, been made a better place because of it. Each one of their names is synonymous with quality and they are famous in their respective industries. Each is still recognised as having been a brilliant entrepreneur who just wouldn't quit.

James Allan reminds us in his book *As a Man Thinketh*, 'The greatest achievement was at first and for a time a dream. The oak sleeps in the acorn; the bird waits in the egg; and in the highest vision of the soul a waking angel stirs. Dreams are the seedlings of realities. Your circumstances may be uncongenial, but they shall not long remain so if you but perceive an ideal and strive to reach it.'

George S. Patton, the Second World War US Army general, once said, 'You have to be single-minded. Drive only for one thing on which you have decided. And if it looks as if you might be getting there, all kinds of people, including some you thought were your loyal friends, will suddenly show up… to trip you, blacken you and break your spirit.' You can't let them do that. You have to commit to your decision and let nothing pull you off course.

Like all successful people, Dabasir *found his own soul when he realized a great truth*' and had the *'wisdom to understand its magic power – where the determination is, the way can be found'*.

HERE'S AN IDEA FOR YOU...

What problem in your life would you like to solve? Whatever it is, the first step is commitment. Forget blaming various people or institutions; there is nothing to be gained from whining. Take responsibility for your situation, regardless of who is to blame, and determination will help you find your own solution.

46 THE IMPORTANCE OF SETTING GOALS

'I, Dabasir, recently returned from slavery in Syria, with determination to pay my debts and become a man of means worthy of respect in my native city of Babylon, do here engrave upon the clay a permanent record of my affairs to guide and assist me in carrying through my high desires.'

DEFINING IDEA...

If you don't know where you are going, you might wind up someplace else.

~ YOGI BERRA

In *The Richest Man in Babylon's* ninth chapter, '*The Clay Tablets From Babylon,*' we hear how Dabasir turned his life around from slavery to respected and wealthy businessman. Dabasir probably didn't realise it at the time but when he wrote his intentions on a clay tablet he was harnessing the power of his mind in what the personal development industry now calls 'goal setting'.

There are many reasons why making a commitment and documenting that commitment will help in its attainment. The first is logical – you have to know where you are aiming for, because otherwise you might end up somewhere completely different. The second reason is actually biological.

There is a part of the brain called the reticular activating system (RAS) which, amongst other things, decides what we pay attention to. The gorilla experiment in Idea 6 already indicates that we don't notice everything in our environment and that what we do notice depends on our focus at any given time. We also know that we are being bombarded with data through our five senses, every minute of the waking day, and that if we were consciously aware of it all we would go insane. We are only consciously aware of what our RAS has deemed important.

Setting a goal allows you to manage that filtration process and engages your most prized possession – your mind. Setting goals rallies the mind's awesome power to bring to your attention situations, circumstances and opportunities that can bring about your goal. If making more money is your goal, then the RAS will scan the environment and make you aware of money-making information and opportunities. The RAS is at work when you decide to buy a particular kind of new car and then suddenly see that same car on every street. The cars were always there; you just didn't notice them before.

Remember in Idea 32 when I talked about becoming a writer? I wasn't trained as a writer and I didn't know how I would get work, but I set the goal anyway. By doing so I informed my RAS to be on the lookout for information and circumstances that would allow me to accomplish that goal. So when I was having an unrelated conversation with a friend I was able to see the opportunity and grab it.

These days a pen and paper can replace clay tablets, but the significance of goal setting is every bit as important today as it was to Dabasir over 8000 years ago.

HERE'S AN IDEA FOR YOU...

Whatever you want to achieve, you need to set SMART goals. They must be Specific, Measurable, As Now, Realistic and Time-framed. For example, a SMART goal around money would be 'It's 17 July 2010 [time]; I earn £200,000 after tax [specific and measurable]'. It's written in the present tense (as now) and is possible (realistic).

47 DABASIR'S DEBT-RECOVERY PLAN

Mathon, the gold lender of Babylon, appears again – offering Dabasir a tried and tested solution for paying off debts and accumulating wealth. *'Two-tenths of all I have earned shall be divided honorably and fairly among those who have trusted me and to whom I am indebted.'*

Dabasir is please to learn that, *'First, the plan doth provide for my future prosperity. Therefore one-tenth of all I earn shall be set aside as my own to keep.'* Perhaps this is the bit that people forget. If all someone's available money is spent keeping debts at bay then feelings of hopelessness can overtake their good efforts. Therefore it is important to stand by the first rule even when paying off debt and pay yourself first.

Dabasir is then told he must learnt to live on less. *'Therefore seven-tenths of all I earn shall be used to provide a home, clothes to wear, and food to eat, with a bit extra to spend, that our lives be not lacking in pleasure and enjoyment.'*

And the remaining two-tenths are used to pay off the debts. Dabasir engraved the names of all the people he owed money to on a clay tablet together with the amount he owed. Then each month he could give his wife seven-tenths, save a tenth and distribute the remaining two-tenths equally amongst his creditors.

This strategy requires that you talk to the people to whom you owe money and negotiate a settlement. Like Dabasir, you may meet some resistance as creditors are impatient for repayment. However, most organisations will appreciate you being upfront and will agree to a repayment schedule. As the debts clear, redistribute the two-tenths of your income to repay the remaining creditors and eventually you will clear the debt. Assuming, of course, that you cut up your credit and store cards and don't add any more to the debt while trying to pay it off – and also assuming you didn't borrow from a door-to-door loan salesman…

In mid-2004 the UK's National Consumer Council (NCC) lodged a 'super complaint' with the Office of Fair Trading against the growing door-to-door lending industry, which is estimated to be worth billions of pounds. The NCC's research found that 80% of borrowers had no idea what interest rate they were paying – which was on average 177%, with some people being charged up to an even more extraordinary 900% interest! Incredibly, these are not dodgy loan-shark operations with baseball bats and balaclavas, but supposedly reputable financial services organisations. As Nobel Prize winner Pearl S. Buck so eloquently says, 'Man was lost if he went to a usurer, for the interest ran faster than a tiger upon him'.

Use Dabasir's simple plan to rid yourself of debt and *'Thus in due time all indebtedness will surely be paid'.*

HERE'S AN IDEA FOR YOU…

If your two-tenths isn't going far enough in clearing your debt quickly, get creative. Look in your wardrobe and find all the items you haven't worn for over a year. Take photos, write enticing descriptions and list them on eBay. Use the money you make to pay off your loans faster.

48 TAKE ACTION

*'One expects the past to speak of romance and adventure –
"Arabian Nights" sort of things. When instead it discloses the
problem of a person named Dabasir to pay off his debts, one
realizes that conditions upon this old world have not changed
as much in five thousand years as one might expect.'*

DEFINING IDEA...

**The time for action is now.
It's never too late to do something.**

~ CARL SANDBURG,
WRITER AND HISTORIAN

In *The Richest Man in Babylon's* Chapter 9 – *'The Clay Tablets From Babylon'* – Clason includes a letter written in 1934 from Alfred Shrewsbury in Nottingham University's Department of Archaeology.

He tells Professor Caldwell of the Babylon excavation how impressed he was at the condition of the tablets he received and how astonished he was to find them containing, amongst other things, advice about repaying debt. Like so many people Alfred Shrewsbury, whether real or fictitious, was a well-educated man with a good job, and yet he and his wife had found themselves in the spiral of debt.

In their ground-breaking book *Millionaire Next Door* Thomas J. Stanley and William D. Danko discovered that most people have it all wrong about wealth. Wealth is not the same as income. If, like Alfred Shrewsbury, you make a good income each year and spend it all, you are not getting wealthier. Wealth is what you accumulate and not what you spend. The authors also discovered that wealth was seldom down to luck, inheritance, advanced degrees or even intelligence – it was the result of hard work, perseverance, planning and, most of all, self-discipline.

Debt is not a class issue. It is an education and information issue. Unfortunately, we are not taught about the catastrophic effects debt has on our ability to create wealth. If our parents struggle with the same issues as we do, then it's unlikely that they will teach us anything positive about money management. The subject is certainly not covered in most schools. We are therefore not armed with the information we need in order to appreciate how damaging debt can be – just look at the door-to-door borrowers who have no idea what interest they are paying on their loans.

What made Alfred Shrewsbury different to most, however, is that he took action on the good advice he received – albeit from ancient Babylon. Needless to say, he was pleasantly surprised at its effectiveness. He was not a young man yet he was able to prosper, *'All this out of my same old check'*, he writes. *'All our debts being gradually paid and at the same time our investment increasing. Besides we get along, financially, even better than before. Who would believe there could be such a difference in results between following a financial plan and just drifting along.'*

He ends the letter *'we would like to extend our personal thanks to that old chap whose plan saved us from our "Hell on Earth".'*

HERE'S AN IDEA FOR YOU...

If you have debts, try Dabasir's plan. Save a tenth of your monthly income, live on seven-tenths – and budget to make sure you do – and pay your debts using the remaining two-tenths. Talk to your creditors about what you are trying to do and ask that they support your efforts; agree on a timescale.

49 WHERE DOES YOUR MONEY GO?

In the final chapter of Clason's little book we meet *'The Luckiest Man in Babylon'. 'Eyeing the young man's rings and earrings, he thought to himself, "He thinks jewels are for men, still he has his grandfather's strong face. But his grandfather wore no such gaudy robes".'*

In this fable we hear of Sharru Nada, the merchant prince of Babylon who is travelling with the arrogant young grandson of his much respected business partner Arad Gula. Hadan Gula, along with his father, has squandered their inheritance and Sharru Nada wants to help him see the error of his ways before it has all gone. Gaudy robes and over-accessorizing are apparently not a new problem and, just as in Babylon, men in modern times are as guilty of these failings as women.

DEFINING IDEA...

I'm not into the money thing. You can only sleep in one bed at a time. You can only eat one meal at a time, or be in one car at a time. So I don't have to have millions of dollars to be happy. All I need are clothes on my back, a decent meal, and a little loving when I feel like it.

~ RAY CHARLES

According to research analysts Mintel, the male-grooming industry in the UK alone was worth a staggering £685 million in 2008 and is set to rise to £821 million in a year's time. Research by Boots indicates that male cosmetics are the fastest growing segment of the cosmetics and beauty industry, growing 800% since 2000. Men are spending £431 million on haircare, aftershave and skincare products. Men's magazines now apply the same pressure towards perfection that women have endured for decades. Trying to look like a sexy footballer (or his wife) is a national obsession. Wanting superstar looks without superstar incomes has consequences. I'm all for guys looking after themselves, but personally I prefer men to be men, and if a guy takes longer to get ready than I do there is something seriously wrong…

The fable talks of the merits of work in creating a fulfilling life and of cutting your coat according to your cloth. Spend within your means. There is nothing wrong with wanting nice things. Sharru Nada too *'liked fine cloth and wore rich and becoming robes. He liked fine animals and sat easily upon his spirited Arabian stallion.'* But he earned the right to those things through hard work and money management. You may not have an immediate hankering for a spirited stallion, but until you can afford the designer gear without using credit, don't buy it. Who cares if you don't have the latest designer accoutrements? If your friends judge you because of the clothes you wear then you need new friends, not a new suit!

Sharru Nada reminds us that true wealth is rarely displayed by the trappings of wealth and that youth and inexperience can often confuse the two, and *'thy grandfather wore no jewels.'* He had created his wealth through hard work while his ungrateful grandson believed *'Work was made for slaves'*.

HERE'S AN IDEA FOR YOU…

When it comes to clothes, spend your money on good, staple items for your wardrobe. Focus on quality rather than price, and remember that something isn't actually better just because it's expensive.

50 WILLING HANDS MAKE MONEY

'But how could he help such a superior youth with his spendthrift ideas and bejeweled hands? Work he could offer in plenty to willing workers, but naught for men who considered themselves too good for work. Yet he owed it to Arad Gula to do something, not a half-hearted attempt.'

Sharru Nada wanted to make the grandson of his friend see sense before his inheritance was completely lost, and so he told him his story and how he had once been a slave…

DEFINING IDEA…

I don't think that work ever really destroyed anybody. I think that lack of work destroys them a hell of a lot more.

~ KATHARINE HEPBURN

In those days you could become a slave for a number of reasons, often through no fault of your own. In Sharru Nada's case, he had paid for his brothers' indiscretions with his freedom and was sold to a slave dealer. There he met a man called Megiddo who impressed upon him the value of work, *'Some men hate it. They make it their enemy. Better to treat it like a friend, make thyself like it. Don't mind because it is hard. If thou thinkest about what a good house thou build, then who cares if the beams are heavy and it is far from the well to carry the water for the plaster. Thou cannot get ahead by shirking.'*

The issues regarding immigration are complicated, and certainly a country the size of the UK faces many challenges because of immigration policy. These problems are, I believe, without doubt largely due to the dizzying array of benefits available to anyone upon arrival. Unlike countries such as Australia where immigrants know there will be no access to benefits for at least two years the UK seems to whip out its cheque book and ask 'how much?'

At the same time people complain about immigrants taking British jobs, and certainly there will be instances of that, but most of the time they are simply taking jobs that the British refuse to do. In a BBC TV documentary *The Poles are Coming*, aired in March 2008, the difference in work ethic was illustrated with devastating effectiveness… One man arriving in Peterborough from Poland was working within twenty-four hours – picking butternut squash for £7.00 an hour. Some of the locals, on the other hand, were picking up their benefits, drinking cans of lager in the middle of the day and bitching about 'foreigners taking all the jobs' – but they didn't want the jobs and obviously *'considered themselves too good for work'*.

Money for nothing is bad for the soul; it makes people lazy and removes their self-respect. As human beings we thrive on being useful, we achieve a sense of purpose and worth from hard work – and it is the best-known cure for a lean purse.

Megiddo reminds us that, *'work, well-done, does good to the man who does it. It makes him a better man'.*

HERE'S AN IDEA FOR YOU…

If you find yourself out of work, do something. Find a local organisation and volunteer your services, help at the local hospital or old people's home. As well as offering a different perspective, you'll feel better – and it could lead to your next position. Employers recognise someone who is willing to go the extra mile.

51 HUMBLE BEGINNINGS STOP NO ONE

'At that, he confided in me. Something I had never suspected. "Thou knowest not that I, also, am a slave. I am in partnership with my master." " Stop," demanded Hadan Gula. "I will not listen to lies defaming my grandfather. He was no slave." His eyes blazed in anger.'

Sharru Nada remained calm. *'I honor him for rising above his misfortune and becoming a leading citizen of Damascus. Art thou, his grandson, cast of the same mold? Art thou man enough to face true facts, or dost thou prefer to live under false illusions?'*

In Clason's book, Sharru Nada, Arad Gula and Dabasir the camel trader had all been slaves but had ended up as wealthy merchants and respected pillars of Babylonian society. We like to assume that successful people had a series of head starts; boxes that were ticked at birth that gave them access to opportunities from which we were excluded. This is comforting because if we accept the truth that no such right exists then we no longer have an excuse for poor performance. In Clason's last fable he is once again emphasising the irrelevance of our past in respect to our future.

There are countless examples of individuals who started from humble beginnings and cast off the expectations of their upbringing to create wealth and success. Duncan Bannatyne is perhaps best known as one of the five entrepreneurs on the panel of UK television's *Dragons' Den*. Although the Sunday Times Rich List 2008 estimated his wealth at £310 million, Bannatyne's business empire started at the age of twenty-nine when he purchased an ice-cream van for £450. Within a few years he had expanded the business and sold it for £28,000. Since then he's been involved in nursing homes, children's nurseries and his is currently the largest independent health club in the UK.

Sir Alan Sugar is also no stranger to the small screen in the UK's version of Donald Trump's hit US TV show, *The Apprentice*. Sir Alan started from humble beginnings in the east end of London and is now estimated to be worth £830 million. He began his business career selling car aerials and electrical goods out of a van he had bought with his savings of £100.

Vision, determination, passion and persistence will dictate your success far more accurately than random circumstance. Clason invites us to consider, *'If a man has in himself the soul of a slave will he not become one no matter what his birth, even as water seeks its level? If a man has within him the soul of a free man, will he not become respected and honored in his own city in spite of his misfortune?'*

HERE'S AN IDEA FOR YOU...

If you think the circumstances of your life preclude you from achieving your dreams, go online and check out the Sunday Times Rich List. Many of the UK's wealthiest individuals did not begin life with a silver spoon in their mouths. If you've nothing to start with, you have nothing to lose – isn't it worth a try?

52 THE IMPORTANCE OF THE ENTREPRENEURIAL SPIRIT

Spurred on by the wise advice of Megiddo, Sharru Nada marketed himself to the local baker at the slave auction: *'He was impressed by my willingness and began bargaining… At last, much to my joy, the deal was closed. I followed my new master away, thinking I was the luckiest man in Babylon.'*

DEFINING IDEA...

Industry is the soul of business and the keystone of prosperity.
~ CHARLES DICKENS

Sharru Nada was taught how to bake by his new master, Nana-naid, and soon he was willingly doing all the work. Sharru Nada suggested that he could bake extra honey cakes and sell them in the streets. The baker agreed, and he was in business. Although he only kept a quarter of his profit, he was happy to be earning anything at all and had sown the seed for his future success.

He demonstrated the most essential ingredient for wealth – an entrepreneurial spirit. Business was, and always will be, the best way to make money. Once made, that money must be invested – but nothing can replace enterprise in the generation of income.

One of the major attractions to business is the tax advantage it offers. If someone is an employee they work first, have the tax deducted from their pay and then receive the remaining amount. If, one day, that person decides to go into business for themselves then the sequence of events shifts. Whether self-employed or a business owner employing staff, he or she would now work and receive money, then deduct all the business expenses and then pay tax. That order can make a huge difference to your ability to create wealth.

People go into business for many reasons. Sometimes the move is initiated from the outside through redundancy or an inability to find alternative employment. In other cases, internal motivation such as disliking the boss, office politics or the clear recognition of a business opportunity can be enough to trigger the change. Often women are drawn to business because it offers them much greater control and an increased flexibility to manage family commitments, or they just get tired of hitting their head on the 'glass ceiling'. Whatever the reason, setting up a business is not for the faint-hearted. But if you can cope with the uncertainty and thrive on calling the shots, then there are few better ways to wealth. Hard work and enterprise are a powerful combination.

Hadan Gula asked, *"Was work my grandfather's secret key to the golden shekels?"* *"It was the only key he had when I first knew him,"* Sharru Nada replied. *"Thy grandfather enjoyed working. The gods appreciated his efforts and rewarded him liberally."*

When Hadan Gula heard the story of how his grandfather had risen to such wealth, he *'pulled the jeweled baubles from his ears and the rings from his fingers. Then reining his horse, he dropped back and rode with deep respect behind the leader of the caravan.'*

HERE'S AN IDEA FOR YOU...

Risk reversal is a great way to build a business. Ask yourself what problem or fear your customers have with your industry and guarantee against it. For example, plumbers rarely turn up when they say they will. A new plumber could promoting his business as 'Guaranteed to arrive on time or it's FREE.'

CONCLUSION

Money is an essential part of life. Unfortunately, along with many of the other really important life skills, we are not taught about it in school. Instead we get trigonometry and Latin… Today few people even know what frugal means, never mind how to practise frugality. Instead we are encouraged to spend today and worry tomorrow. And worry we do. According to the Samaritans, the suicide rate in the UK peaks in mid-January every year as the Christmas credit card bill thumps onto the doormat. Yes, money is important but it's never that important.

Clason's little book is full of insights and wisdom about the eradication of debt and the accumulation of wealth. And whilst the fable and characters may change, the central messages do not. Those messages are succinctly articulated in Chapter 5 – 'The Five Laws of Gold'.

THE FIVE LAWS OF GOLD

I. Gold cometh gladly and in increasing quantity to any man who will put by not less than one-tenth of his earnings to create an estate for his future and that of his family.

II. Gold laboreth diligently and contentedly for the wise owner who finds for it profitable employment, multiplying even as the flocks of the field.

III. Gold clingeth to the protection of the cautious owner who invests it under the advice of men wise in its handling.

IV. Gold slippeth away from the man who invests it in businesses or purposes with which he is not familiar or which are not approved by those skilled in its keep.

V. Gold flees the man who would force it to impossible earnings or who followeth the alluring advice of tricksters and schemers or who trusts it to his own inexperience and romantic desires in investment.

To him who is without knowledge of the five laws, gold comes not often, and goeth away quickly. But to him who abides by the five laws, gold comes and works as his dutiful slave.

For a book about wealth, Clason's fables often talk more about ethics and morality than they do about money. He is obviously keen to point out that money is just a means to an end and not the end itself. Wealth accumulation is a noble pursuit when the intention behind it is a desire to be of service, to work hard and add value so that you and your loved ones can be financially secure. There is, however, nothing noble about avarice when the accumulation of wealth matters at the cost of all else.

When is enough, enough? At what point do outrageous, unnecessary and narcissistic displays of wealth become offensive? There is an unspoken competition, for example, to own the world's biggest yacht. The money spent on this ego-driven one-upmanship could probably save millions of lives in Africa through the supply of malaria tablets – and with change left over! At what point should people who waste money trying to disprove the inverted relationship between the size of their yacht and the size of their penis offend us? What sort of society have we created when such excess is admired instead of ridiculed?

Whether you find yourself stressed and miserable because your debt has got out of hand or whether you just want to work out how to secure your financial future, *The Richest Man in Babylon* could indeed be your salvation. It won't happen overnight but if you start now and make sure you teach your kids its lessons, then perhaps you can help to distribute the world's wealth a little more equitably.

REFERENCE MATERIAL

IDEA 1
Unlimited Power by Anthony Robbins, p. 19

IDEA 3
The 75 Greatest Management Decisions ever made … and some of the worst
by Stuart Crainer, p. 224

IDEA 4
Three Steps to Wealth and Power by Christopher Howard, pp. 78–9

IDEA 6
'Invisible gorilla steals Ig Nobel prize' by Jeff Hecht, *New Scientist*, 1 October 2004

IDEA 7
'Rags to riches: The lottery winner who blew his £10 million jackpot – and is now £2 million in debt' by Chris Brooke, *Daily Mail*, 11 February 2008

IDEA 8
The Rise and Fall… and Rise Again by Gerald Ratner

IDEA 11
Think and Grow Rich by Napoleon Hill
'*Britain's Got Talent*' website, 2008 Competition
As A Man Thinketh by James Allen

IDEA 12
Seven Strategies for Wealth and Happiness by Jim Rohn, p. 12

IDEA 13
'*Key Facts about The National Lottery*', Camelot Press Office, 31 March 2007
'IMF: $1T In Subprime losses' by Paul Tharp, *New York Post*, April 9 2008

IDEA 14
'Billionaires and their taxes' by Nick Louth, *Money*, 14 September 2007
'Check your tax code you may be entitled to a refund', *Bytestart website*
'Have you paid too much tax through PAYE?', *Direct.gov.uk website*

IDEA 15
'Debt Facts and Figures – Compiled 1st February 2008', *Credit Action website*

IDEA 16
'Debt Facts and Figures – Compiled 1st February 2008', *Credit Action website*

IDEA 17
'*Key Facts about The National Lottery*', Camelot Press Office, 31 March 2007

IDEA 18.
'*This is red button*' *website*

IDEA 19
'The Endowments Problem', *Which? website*
'Q&A: Endowment mortgage shortfall', *BBC news website*

IDEA 22
'Nigeria scams "cost UK billions"', *BBC news website*, 20 November 2006
'Turning the tables on Nigeria's e-mail conmen' by Dan Damon, *BBC News website*, 13 July 2004

IDEA 24
'Borrowing six times your salary' by Faith Archer, *Daily Telegraph*, 14 April 2007

IDEA 27
'Barclays chief brands credit cards a rip-off' by Andrew Cave,
Daily Telegraph, 17 October 2003
'Debt Facts and Figures – Compiled 1st February 2008', *Credit Action website*
'Money Sickness Syndrome could affect almost half the UK population', *Axa Media Centre Press Release*, 20 January 2006

IDEA 28
'*The Tax Guide*' *website*

IDEA 29
'Just why are the British so stingy?' by Richard Morrison, *Times Online*, 20 February 2008
'False charity: is our generosity being wasted?' by Nic Cicutti, *MSN Money*, April 12 2007
'Warren Buffett gives away his fortune' by Carol J Loomis, *Fortune Magazine*, June 25 2006

IDEA 30
The Underground History of American Education by John T Gatto

IDEA 31
British Gambling Prevalence Survey 2007, National Centre for Social Research
Report: Gambling or Gaming Entertainment Or Exploitation? The Church of England Ethical Investment Advisory Group, February 2003

IDEA 32
Google corporate website – corporate history information

IDEA 33
Google corporate website – corporate history information

IDEA 34
'Bad heir day: Paris Hilton to inherit just £2.5 million as grandfather pledges bulk of fortune to charity', *Daily Mail online*, 29 December 2007
'Handing it down' by Finlo Rohrer, *BBC News Magazine*, 30 January 2008

IDEA 35
'Le Rogue Trader: Financial world left stunned by £3.7bn fraud' by John Lichfield, *Independent*, 25 January 2008

IDEA 36
'On this day', *BBC News*, 19 October 1987

IDEA 37
'Headmaster hanged himself after racking up online gambling debts', *Daily Mail Online*, 20 September 2007
'Online bingo jackpot is on the cards' by Matthew Goodman, *Sunday Times*, 20 May 2007
'Online poker addict jailed for a year' by Simon de Bruxelles, *The Times*, 31 December 2005

IDEA 41
'Credit Suisse expects to post quarterly loss after "misconduct" by traders' by Susanne Fowler, *International Herald Tribune*, March 20, 2008
'Credit Suisse fuels fear of new wave of losses' by Nick Clark, *Independent*, 21 February 2008
'Mervyn King: Banks paying price for their greed' by Gary Duncan and Grainne Gilmore, *The Times*, 30 April 2008

IDEA 43
The Science of Getting Rich by Wallace D. Wattles, Chapter 9

IDEA 44
'Runaway debts leave thousands high and dry', *Daily Telegraph*, 26 July 2006
Speaker's Library of Business Stories Anecdotes and Humour by Joe Griffith, p. 29

IDEA 45
The Science of Getting Rich by Wallace D. Wattles, Chapter 9
Speaker's Library of Business Stories Anecdotes and Humour by Joe Griffith, p. 93
As a Man Thinketh by James Allen

IDEA 46
Unleash the Giant Within by Anthony Robbins, p. 289

IDEA 47
'Doorstep lenders under scrutiny', *BBC news channel*, 14 June, 2004

IDEA 48
The Millionaire Next Door by Thomas J Stanley PhD and William D Danko PhD, p. 2

IDEA 49
'Who said beauty is only for women?' by Sarah Howden, *Scotsman*, 12 June 2008

IDEA 50
'The £7-per-hour jobs locals don't want', *BBC news channel*, 11 March 2008

INDEX

23837129R00071

Printed in Great Britain
by Amazon